MISSION POSSIBLE

mission
POSSIBLE

creating a mission
for work and life

Maureen F. Fitzgerald

Quinn Publishing
2003

NATIONAL LIBRARY OF CANADA CATALOGUING IN PUBLICATION DATA

Fitzgerald, Maureen F
    Mission possible: creating a mission for work and life / Maureen F. Fitzgerald

ISBN 0-9732451-0-7

1. Self-actualization (Psychology) 2. Success—Psychological aspects. 3. Goal (Psychology) 1. Title.
BF637.S4F575 2003   158.1   C2003-910131-2

Layout and design: The Vancouver Desktop Publishing Centre
Cover design: Lee Edward Fodi
Cover photo: Reine Mihtla
Proofreading: Naomi Pauls
Printed and bound in Canada at Friesens

Excerpts from *Winner Instinct: The 6 New Laws of Success*, copyright 1999 by Lesley Bendaly, reprinted by permission of HarperCollins Publishers Ltd.

Excerpts from *Creating True Prosperity* by Shakti Gawain, reprinted by permission of New World Library, Novato CA 94949.

Excerpts from *It's Not About the Bike*, copyright 1997 by Lance Armstrong, reprinted by permission of G.P. Putnam's Sons, a division of Penguin Group (USA).

Excerpts from *Take Your Soul to Work* by Tanis Helliwell, copyright 1999 by Tanis Helliwell, reprinted by permission of Random House Canada and Adams Media (USA).

Best attempts were made at obtaining permissions. The publisher will be happy to remedy any oversights.

To Monica, my best friend

You cannot change the wind, but you can adjust your sails.
—Anonymous

Contents

Introduction: The Power of Mission   15

People with a mission live with a sense of purpose and direction. They achieve success by aligning their uniqueness with their work. In this chapter you will learn the difference between a vision and a mission and the importance of both. You will be introduced to the five strategies to finding your mission: creating your vision, identifying your vessel, developing your mission statement, selecting your goals and taking action.

Strategy 1: Creating Your Vision   37

The first step in developing your mission is creating a vision of where you want to be in the future. A vision is your description of an ideal life or your personal definition of success. In this chapter you will learn how to create your own vision through a variety of techniques. You will learn about the components and forms of a vision statement and will create your own personal vision statement.

Strategy 2: Identifying Your Unique Vessel   61

In order to align yourself with your work, you must know who you are and what motivates you. Your skills, abilities and interests are the equipment or vessel that will help you to achieve your vision. In this chapter you will learn about the three aspects of your vessel: your assets, your approach and your ambitions. You will use a series of techniques to identify your particular uniqueness and your unique vessel.

Your mission is your reason for being. It flows from your vision and vessel and provides a purpose and direction for your life and work. It can be used as a beacon and a measure of success. In this chapter you will learn about the three parts of a mission statement: action, audience and accomplishment. You will learn a unique way to develop and write your own mission statement.

Your goals describe the specific way in which you will achieve your mission. They describe what you will do, how you will do it and when. In this chapter you will learn how to decide what you want to do in life and work—from a multitude of possibilities. You will select your goals and strategies through a strategic planning process. You will identify your strengths, weaknesses, opportunities and threats and learn how to evaluate your progress.

Armed with your vision, vessel, mission and goals you will be in a position to take action and implement your strategies. This involves seeking opportunities and addressing challenges. This chapter introduces five strategies to help ensure your vision becomes a reality. You will learn how to integrate your vision and mission, identify supports, adopt appropriate attitudes, face your fears and stay focussed.

Conclusion: Living your Mission

This chapter includes an overview of the five strategies presented in this book. You will also find four blank cue cards so that you can record your vision, vessel, mission and goals—and carry them with you.

Preface

This book will help you become successful at work and in life. You will learn how to maximize your potential and take control of your life.

You will develop a clearer sense of your uniqueness and how that translates into your career, business and life. This book will show you how to create a focus and vision for your life. You will learn how to:

- Create your personal vision;
- Identify your particular uniqueness;
- Develop your own mission statement;
- Select goals and strategies for fulfilling your mission; and
- Implement your mission, overcome obstacles and integrate your mission into your life.

You will learn through the stories of those who have created, and are now living, their missions. You will end up with a concrete action plan to bring about your vision and mission.

Creating your vision and mission and integrating them into your life will bring about the following results:

- You will love what you do;
- Your work will seem easy;
- You will be excited and energized by your work;
- You will be able to motivate others to help you;
- You will make the money you think you deserve; and
- You will love your life.

Before beginning this book you will find it useful to take a quick measure of where you are right now. This way you will be able to see your improvements after completing the book and beginning to live a life that is more consistent with your uniqueness. Circle the number that reflects how you feel right now. One rates low and five rates high.

1. Are you happy and healthy?

I am healthy	1	2	3	4	5
I have sufficient energy to do what I want	1	2	3	4	5
I laugh often	1	2	3	4	5
I feel at peace	1	2	3	4	5
I am generally content	1	2	3	4	5

2. Do you have good relations?

I have supportive relationships	1	2	3	4	5
I like the people I work with	1	2	3	4	5
I am excited about going to work	1	2	3	4	5
I feel I am adding value and my work is worthwhile	1	2	3	4	5
I feel my work is compatible with my values and beliefs	1	2	3	4	5

3. Do you have sufficient resources?

I have enough money to meet my needs	1	2	3	4	5
I am living my dreams	1	2	3	4	5
I feel free to make choices	1	2	3	4	5
I have time to spend on myself	1	2	3	4	5
I am continually growing and learning	1	2	3	4	5

4. Do you have a sense of meaning?

I feel I am making a difference	1	2	3	4	5
I am proud to tell others where I work	1	2	3	4	5
I feel good when my work is complete	1	2	3	4	5
I feel I am contributing in a meaningful way	1	2	3	4	5
I am fairly confident and assertive	1	2	3	4	5

There are no right answers. At a very personal level you know those areas of your life that need to be improved.

This book is about taking action rather than simply adopting a philosophy or learning some tips about how to be better. Follow the step-by-step process in the following chapters and it will change your life.

If not now, when?

INTRODUCTION
The Power of Mission

*Choose a job you love and you will never
have to work a day in your life.*
—Confucius

This book is about being extraordinarily successful in work and life. We all dream of happiness and success. We all have ideas about what we will do when we have "made it." We all want to feel as though we make a difference and that our lives are important.

For many of us, these ideals have been taken over by circumstance. We are often surprised to find ourselves in careers and situations that have never been that great. We tell ourselves that someday we will get back on track. Some of us secretly hope that we will be downsized so we can finally get on with our lives in the way in which we imagined. Each day we put off the decision to begin living our lives. Worse still, many of us silently hope that each Monday is a Friday and wish most of our lives away. We tell ourselves that one day we will do what we love. But often that day comes too late.

My aim for this book is to inspire you to do what you love and provide you with the practical tools to do so. My only hope is that you begin to better see who you are and to align your uniqueness with your life and work. I want you to learn from me and those whom I have helped that if you focus on your unique genius, you will transform your life and work.

Everyone knows someone who loves what they do. These individuals are energized and excited about going to work. They continually come up with new ideas, attract good things and seem to have boundless energy. Yet they also have a confidence surrounding them that exudes a sense of peace. They are busy but not rushed, strategic but not overly competitive. They have a deeper sense that what they are doing is useful and therefore tend to work in a purposeful way. Best of all, their energy is contagious and they seem to be surrounded by supportive people. For them, resources and money appear to come easily. This can be you.

My story

I have had four careers and about twenty jobs. Although I am a lawyer and consultant now, I worked for many years in jobs that were not always right for me. I often started out feeling inspired and motivated, but eventually outgrew each job. Recalling the last corporate law position I held, I wonder why I stayed so long. I loved my work and enjoyed my colleagues, but I can vividly recall the increasing sense of frustration as I began to outgrow my job. I became less tolerant with people and resented requests that demanded particular effort. It was the slippery slope toward mediocrity.

Luckily I have "low corporate pain threshold." This means that I am not very good at working at jobs that do not inspire me. When I get bored, I either look for another project or another job. This "problem" has served me very well in my current life as a

> *If you are called to be a street sweeper, sweep streets even as Michelangelo painted, or Beethoven composed music, or Shakespeare wrote poetry. Sweep streets so well that all the hosts of heaven and earth will pause to say, "Here lived a great street sweeper who did his job well."*
>
> —Martin Luther King, Jr.

consultant and coach. I understand the human need to grow and contribute and can help individuals break out of mediocrity and create a fuller life.

In 1999, after ten years of law practice, I decided to change my life. I wish I could say it was easy, but that would not be completely accurate. The good news is that I am now where I was clearly meant to be and that you, by reading this book, can find out where you are meant to be.

As I was working in my office one day, a colleague peeked in and asked how I was. I looked up from my foot-deep files and noticed that she really meant it. She actually cared about me and was interested in how I was doing. Although my usual response was a prompt "Just fine, how about you" for some reason, on that particular day I said, "Not very good." She quietly shut the door, walked over to me, and placed an arm around my shoulders. I began sobbing. She looked me straight in the eye and said, "Maureen, you must go home now and take some time off." I packed up my briefcase and never returned.

After that day, I decided that I would never again work in a job that I did not like and would only work with people who brought out the best in me. I began reading everything I could get my hands on that related to careers, entrepreneurs, purpose in life, and well-being. But there was no book that dealt with my particular situation. I needed a quick way to set up a consulting practice but I had no idea about the area. As a lawyer, facilitator, writer and mediator, I could do a million different things. It was not until I created my own personal mission statement that I realized what was missing. *None of the books that I read asked what I considered to be the three most important questions: what is extraordinarily*

> *Fulfilling our purpose is key to success in the new economy. Being on purpose . . . allows us to cope with the stressors: heavy loads and long hours, the overlapping of work and personal lives, and the need to perform at our peak in order to compete. But in addition, purpose is a deep desire that each of us longs to fill.*
> —Leslie Bendaly,
> *Winner Instinct*

unique about you? what do you care deeply about? and how do you align this with your life and work?

I created a workshop and began coaching entrepreneurs, consultants and executives about how to align their uniqueness with their work. The feedback from the participants and my clients was amazing. The following are some of the comments: "Thank you, Maureen, for giving me permission to do what I love." "I realized that I always knew what my mission was, but for some reason did not see it." "I am now so clear about where I am going and I am so excited." "I no longer feel like I am on a conveyor belt of endless tasks and projects; I know where I am going and how I will get there." I was touched by their comments, and their feedback inspired me to write this book.

I now have a successful practice helping organizations prevent workplace problems from becoming legal issues and also pursuing a doctorate. I feel blessed to have been given the gift of writing so that I can share my learning with others. I truly hope that your journey is smoother as a result.

From a very young age I have believed that each of us is like a piece in an ever-evolving jigsaw puzzle. We can expand and contract. Each of us has a role to play or an impact to make in this world. And we each touch others. Our lives, therefore, consist of being the best we can be given our circumstances and making the best of what we have.

You have only two choices

About twenty years ago research was conducted on how people got rich. The researchers asked 1500 people what they planned to do in their career. The vast majority of participants (about 80%) said that they intended to go out and make enough money so that they could someday quit their jobs and then do what they really wanted to do. The remainder of the participants planned to work at what they loved and worry about the money later. After twenty years, 101 of the 1500 participants had become millionaires. All but one came from the group who had decided to pursue their passion.

Many people work at jobs and run businesses that they do not like. They do not believe that they can make money doing what they love and therefore simply put in hour after hour at work without interest or energy. Some people believe that they must struggle in life by doing hard work. They work in order to earn the money necessary to live on weekends and holidays.

Many people move through life without much reflection. Some let events and circumstances control what they do. These people tend to believe that what happens to them is beyond their control and often blame unfortunate circumstances on chance or bad luck. A lot of these people

There is a time in every man's education when he arrives at the conviction that . . . imitation is suicide; that he must take himself for better or worse as his portion; that though the wide universe is full of good, no kernel of nourishing can come to him but through his toil bestowed on that plot of ground which is given to him to till. The power which resides in him is new in nature, and nor but he knows what that is which he can do, nor does he know until he has tried. . . . Trust thyself: every heart vibrates to that iron string.
—Ralph Waldo Emerson

wonder late in life whether they might have been able to live their lives differently.

Others believe that life should be lived with zest. They do not think that work is necessarily hard or distasteful. These people believe that they are fundamentally valuable and that they have a contribution to make. They believe that they only have one life to live and tend to live that life with a sense of meaning, believing that the world is full of opportunities and that what they do is important. Taking responsibility for the good and bad that happens in their lives, these people realize that they are unique and believe they have an important role to play. They tend to be at peace when they approach death, knowing that they did their best and lived a full life.

No matter what you think now, your life is of great consequence. What you do or don't do contributes in many significant ways—to you, to those you come in contact with, and even to the entire world. You really only have two choices: to live your life in a conscious and directed way with purpose and meaning, or to live your life as a victim of circumstance.

Joe Matas came to see me last October. He had decided to set up a shoe shop in a very expensive district in a major city. He excitedly told me that he had secured a location through his uncle who was a real estate agent and had got a deal on the monthly rental fee. Joe had been a sales manager in a number of retail outlets and was tired of others profiting from his retail expertise. He was not experienced in the shoe industry, but was a quick learner.

Finding a mission and then fulfilling it is perhaps the most vital activity in which a person can engage.
—Richard Leider and David A. Shapiro, Repacking Your Bags

I asked him why he wanted to sell shoes. He told me that the markup on shoes was about 100% and it was a quick way to make a lot of money. When I asked if he liked shoes, he said, "No." When I asked if he had an interest in the fashion industry, he said, "No." When I asked if he had any interest in feet or women, he said, "No." So I said to him: "Let's say for a moment that the location next to your shoe shop becomes vacant and a new shoe shop opens up. Let's say that the owner is an entrepreneur from a family of Italian shoe manufacturers. Let's say the owner has a passion for fashion, loves women, loves feet, loves leather, and loves people. What might be the difference between you and her? I suspect that her passion for her job will be reflected in all aspects of her business, from her hours of work to her conversations with her clients. Although I have no idea who will be the more profitable in a monetary sense, I would venture that if you chose a business that inspired you, you would be successful in ways that you had not yet contemplated."

> *Far better it is to dare mighty things, to win glorious triumphs even though checkered by failure, than to rank with those poor spirits who neither enjoy nor suffer much because they live in the gray twilight that knows neither victory nor defeat.*
> —Theodore Roosevelt

Each and every person is unique. We each have particular skills, abilities and interests. In our lives we each have a particular role to play, journey to take and contribution to make. We have unique opportunities at particular times in our lives that no one else has. If we focus on what is best about ourselves and put it to proper use, we will excel and also be happy. At the same time we will rise up to our highest purpose and receive the greatest joy. We were not put on earth to suffer. Although life can be hard, there is no point in making it harder by doing something that is inconsistent with our fundamental nature.

Every one of us has been given a capacity to succeed and is confronted with a host of opportunities in our lives. If you are able to identify your unique gifts and put them to best use, you will not only be happy, but you can use them in a way that is most appropriate.

Sometimes the best path for us is also the easiest path. Those who find what they love may continue working hard but will not feel as though they are working.

So how do you begin to work and live in a conscious way that is truly consistent with who you are? The answer is through the development of a vision, a mission and goals. In doing so you will find the path that you were born to follow and will be more able to take advantage of opportunities and face challenges on your journey.

What is a vision? What is a mission?

Victor Frankl, an Austrian psychologist who survived the death camps of Nazi Germany, discovered that the single most significant factor impacting survival in the camps was a sense of future vision—the impelling conviction of those who were to survive that they had a mission to perform.

A vision and a mission are not the same. A vision is an

ultimate and ideal destiny. It is your ideal future state. A vision is a dream that can really only be measured at the end of your life, when it has been achieved.

A mission describes what you must do to reach this vision. A mission identifies what you wish to achieve, who you intend to focus on, and how you will accomplish your vision. A mission is often used to measure personal and professional success.

Together, a vision and a mission provide a beacon or direction to keep you on course and give you focus. Both your vision and your mission reflect a uniqueness that is not shared by any two individuals or groups.

> *Everyone has his own specific vocation or mission in life; everyone must carry out a concrete assignment that demands fulfillment. Therein, he cannot be replaced, nor can his life be repeated. Thus everyone's task is [as] unique as his specific opportunity to implement it.*
> —Victor Frankl

Why visions and missions are important now

Missions are particularly important at this point in history. Because of the changes in the workplace and the way in which work is being done, individuals and businesses need to have a sense of direction and be able to manage their lives and work more than ever.

Here are some trends that reflect changes in the population, the market and in workplaces.

Trend 1: Baby boomers hit midlife

The main group impacting the workplace and society is the baby boomers, who now have an average age of about forty-seven. This means that most are well established in their careers, their children will soon be leaving home, and they are increasingly aware of their health and mortality. They have a general awareness that good physical and mental health can lead to longevity.

Psychologists call this midlife and recognize that many adults at this point in their development will begin to question why they are doing what they are doing. At the same time, baby boomers feel there is an increasing need to make a difference or leave a legacy.

Many autobiographies have been written about people who, confronted with death, shift their careers and redirect their entire lives. One such book was written by Lance Armstrong, a famous American cyclist who, at the peak of his career, was diagnosed with cancer. He faced extraordinary adversity, but rose above it to win another Tour de France.

Many people in this age group are increasingly dissatisfied with their work and will begin to consider other options. Many will quit their regular jobs and set up their own businesses or become consultants.

This is the age of increasing self-actualization. Boomers will no longer tolerate mediocre jobs and will become more involved in things that they feel will have

> *Everybody's favorite question is "How did cancer change you?" The real question is, how didn't it change me? I left my house on October 2, 1996 as one person and came home as another. I was a world class athlete with a mansion on a river bank, keys to a Porsche, and a self-made future in the bank. I was one of the top riders in the world and my career was moving along a perfect arc of success. I returned a different person, literally. In a way, the old me died, and I was given a second life.*
>
> —Lance Armstrong,
> *It's Not About the Bike—
> My Journey Back to Life*

an impact. Fewer people seem able to cope with corporate pain. This generation is becoming less tolerant of workplaces that are not consistent with their internal values.

Trend 2: The cultural creatives

The baby boomers form part of a larger trend that has been labeled as the renaissance age or the age of the "cultural creatives." In 2000, Paul Ray and Sherry Anderson pulled together thirteen years of research and identified this subculture. About fifty million people in North America care about ecology and social justice, relationships and spirituality.

If there is any phrase that captures the new thinking about work, it's take it personally. Work is no longer experienced as an impersonal force of nature over which one has no control. Instead people are asking, indeed demanding, that work meet their personal needs.
—Barbara Moses, The Good News About Careers

This generation is searching for meaning at work and in life. Barbara Moses, a career expert, believes that people are no longer willing to work in ways that are inconsistent with who they really are and that they require more authenticity at work.

Trend 3: Increasing self-employment

This is the generation of self-employment. Recent statistics indicate that the largest growth area in business is in small business. More and more people are recognizing the value of consulting and realizing that there is no such thing as job security. At the same time, corporations are contracting out services as never before to enable them to remain flexible in global markets. Companies no longer hire employees in jobs for life, and they expect internal employees to view themselves as contractors or consultants.

> *Wretchedly soulless work is rampant, and, thanks to an increase in spiritual awareness and personal development, people no longer want to be part of an organization that is not responsible socially and environmentally. Many more people want to make a difference, not just a living.*
> —Jack Canfield and Jacqueline Miller, Heart at Work

The age of long-term jobs has disappeared. In his book *Creating You & Co.*, William Bridges, described the difference between old jobs and new jobs in the following way:

Jobs minimized the differences between individual workers. What you or I wanted was irrelevant. We each had talents we'd never used, but that didn't matter because no one really believed that the average job gave you a chance to express yourself. The fact that you were really temperamentally better suited to a kind of work other than what we did was . . . well, one of those unfortunate things that happen in the world of work. . . . In the dejobbed world, the truth that each of us has an inherent lifework is suddenly rich with meaning. Nothing less than finding what you were meant to be and do will give you the motivation and the capability that today's work world demands. Identifying your lifework is no longer an escapist fantasy. It is a condition for being successful. You now have to discover your lifework if you are to have a chance of creating a satisfactory and satisfying work life.

In the past, if employees possessed the required qualifications, not much attention was paid to whether they were working in a way that was consistent with who they were.

As the old hierarchies give way, individuals gain more influence and control over what they do and work under less supervision. Because more employees work as consultants, they need, more than ever, to be aware of their particular skills and abilities. They must have a sense of career direction and a "portfolio" or bundle of attributes that they can offer to each of the projects, jobs or businesses in which they become engaged.

At the same time, the role of managers has changed substantially. They are taking on roles as mentors, coaches and mediators and require entirely different skills than their predecessors. These managers empower employees to be their best by aligning individual and corporate goals and getting out of the way. They expect individuals to know their own abilities and goals and trust them to understand their role and the skills they each bring to a project. The way in which employees are measured is in terms of outcomes or results. The trends impacting workplaces look something like this:

> *The reason so many people from the baby-boom generation are suffering from midlife crisis is because they never pursued a job or career that was their passion. During the 1980s, most of these people pursued careers or jobs that paid the most money, so they could live the yuppie lifestyle of excess materialism. They may have achieved career success as they defined the term. They got to the top of the corporate ladder and acquired their material possessions. However, their marriages may be in the shambles, their children are all messed up, and they themselves are suffering from excessive stress and dissatisfaction.*
> *—Ernie J. Zelinski,*
> *The Joy of Thinking Big*

Old workplace	New workplace
Top down	Bottom up
Employees	Internal consultants

Teamwork	Collaboration
Managing	Leading and motivating
Job descriptions	Competencies
Departments	Floating project teams
Fear	Trust and relationships
Structure	Feedback systems and outcomes
Stability	Living organisms
No change	Constant change

These changes place pressure on individuals to manage themselves in ways they have not had to in the past. They must have a sense of direction and understand how their goals align with their clients. They must possess a clear vision and mission with associated goals and strategies.

The benefits of a mission statement

A mission statement is important in many ways and can be used for a variety of purposes. At its best, a mission statement forces you to ask the questions: what do you want to do? and who do you want to be? It will help you identify what is best about you and enable you to align what you love with your work.

If you don't care about where you are going, any direction will do.
—Anonymous

Even if you already have a mission statement, it may not be working well for you. *The ultimate goal in creating a mission is to design one that is useful to you.* It is only relevant to the extent to which you can use it in a constructive manner. There are, however, four specific benefits of a mission statement: to provide direction, to describe you and your work, to measure your success and to increase your sense of well-being.

Benefit 1: A mission statement provides direction

A mission statement will provide you with a direction and a beacon. It will act as both an end-point and a compass. This means that it will help you stay on track.

It will assist you in making life and career decisions. For example, it will help you decide whether to accept a new job or to take on a new contract or project. It will help you in deciding what you should do, but also, perhaps more importantly, it will help you decide what you should not do. If you are aware of your mission you will be less likely to take on projects that are inconsistent with your values or direction.

When you are in the midst of confusion and chaos you will be able to refocus with the help of your mission statement. It can be your guiding light. It will help you set your goals and priorities.

Benefit 2: A mission statement describes what you do

A mission statement describes what you do and who you are. It will provide clarity about who you are—for yourself, your clients, your supporters, your employees and all those who come in contact with you. It can also describe your particular approach and values.

It will help you in describing your

> *The idea of a permanent job is obsolete. Your job today is never safe! The work world is in constant turmoil. . . . You must be prepared to go job hunting for the rest of your life. No one owes you a job—not your present employer, not your union, not even if you work for Mom and Dad. It's up to you to create your future. In the 21st century, almost everyone up through the highest ranks of professionals will feel increased pressure to package themselves as a marketable "portfolio" of talents.*
>
> *—Richard Leider and David A. Shapiro, Repacking Your Bags*

> *Whether you are naturally level headed, spontaneously enthusiastic, artlessly charming or born to pressure, we take our behaviors with us into everything we do. If what you do is at the core of who you are, your stress level will go down.*
>
> —Dr. Harry Levinson

services and marketing yourself. Although you might think that you are competing against others, niche marketing demands that you focus on those things that make you unique. In doing so you will create a place where you are not competing directly with anyone.

You will also be able to identify those situations when you are the best person to do the job, or when it might be better for someone else to do the work.

Benefit 3: A mission statement measures your success

A mission statement provides a tool to assess the extent to which you are successful. It describes where you are going and thus can be used to measure when you have arrived. When you feel overwhelmed, a mission statement can give you a sense of perspective and remind you of your ultimate objectives. It is a source of inspiration and motivation.

If you work with others or have employees, it will give them a sense of their contribution. At the end of the day you will have a better sense of accomplishment and increased motivation to continuously improve.

Benefit 4: A mission statement increases well-being

A mission statement can help reduce stress and enhance well-being. It helps you identify your personal values and interests so that you can ultimately align your work with your passion. But it does much more. It also gives you a sense of purpose and a sense of control.

David Whyte, in his book *Crossing the Unknown Sea*, tells us that finding meaning or purpose to work is crucial to an overall sense of well-being. Organizations that excel often encourage their workers to question what they are doing.

It is a proven fact that dedicated employees have reduced absenteeism, improved morale, less stress and less heart disease.

Victor Frankl discovered that personal pleasure or happiness did not motivate human beings. Rather it was the "will to meaning," or working toward finding meaning in life. He found that happiness was a by-product of the search for meaning, not the end product. There is no shortcut to happiness. For Frankl, meaningful work and meaningful love were more important than self-interest.

Research shows that people who feel that their abilities are not being utilized on the job or who feel that their work is boring have a higher risk of heart disease than those who feel their skills are being put to best use.

> *People are becoming self-employed because their self-esteem is in good order and they want to learn more about what they can be as human beings. For a lot of them, that's connected to a vision of a different kind of world they'd like to build. I see this as the most powerful force in entrepreneurship and a tremendous source of commitment.*
> —Barbara Winter, *Making a Living without a Job*

When to create a mission

It is never too early or too late to begin thinking about your mission—and there is no best time to create a mission statement. If you are a particularly reflective person, you may have contemplated your mission in your teens. Many people begin to think about their direction in life when they enter the work

> *It is the denial of death that is particularly responsible for people living empty purposeless lives; for when you live as if you will live forever, it becomes too easy to postpone things you know that you must do. You live your life in preparation for tomorrow or in remembrance of yesterday, and meanwhile each day is lost.*
>
> —Elisabeth Kubler-Ross

world—often upon graduation from university. This is because the exercise of finding employment involves looking at your particular interests and abilities and matching these to an appropriate job or career. In their desperation to find jobs, many graduates do not spend sufficient time identifying their uniqueness and finding the "ideal" job.

Many people do not actually think about the purpose of their lives until they are in the midst of a transition or crisis. Although transitions can occur at various times in life, they are often linked to significant life events such as marriage, changes in jobs, divorce or childbirth. At these times people are more receptive to asking the bigger questions about life. It is quite common for people between the ages of thirty-five and fifty-five to begin to think about their life direction. Many people in this age group have built a career foundation, but may have outgrown their particular career. They are often looking for a way to make a difference.

The process of creating your mission can be enormously powerful when you are in the midst of a transition. During a transition you are able to step off the treadmill of life and reflect, open up spaces, and free up your mind to question what you have been doing so far and why—without feeling compelled to rationalize.

Thinking about a mission statement is critical when contemplating a career change. Those who spend time reflecting on who they are and what they want to achieve will be better able to align their work with their uniqueness. Indeed, it would be odd for someone to start a new job or business without some clarity about where they wanted to go, both personally and professionally.

Many people do not discover what they want to do until later in life. Regardless of how old or young you are, or what you have done so far, it is never too late to discover your mission and pursue it. Barbara Sher, an expert in career and life transitions, gave the following title to her most recent book: *It's only too late if you don't start now*. So, do it now.

How to create a mission statement

The process of creating your vision and mission involves identifying what you want in life and focussing on what is unique about you. It is about aligning your uniqueness with your life and work by creating a mission statement that is specific to you and your circumstances. In this book I introduce the following five strategies:

1. Create your vision
2. Identify your unique vessel
3. Develop your mission statement
4. Select your goals and strategies
5. Take action

Each of these strategies is covered in the following chapters.

> If corporations truly want their employees to be entrepreneurial—to be passionate, creative, innovative and excited about their work—they must meet the challenge of encouraging employees to express their passion. Entrepreneur—leaders must recognize the need to look at their workers as individuals with hearts, talents and ideas and must find ways to encourage workers to bring their personal passions to bear on their work.
>
> —Ann Coombs,
> *The Living Workplace*

> *There is vitality, a life force, a quickening that is translated through you into action—and because there is only one of you in all time, this expression is unique. And if you block it, it will never exist through any other medium and will be lost. The world will not have it. It is not your business to determine how good it is, nor how valuable it is, nor how it compares with other expressions. It is your business to keep it yours clearly and directly, to keep the channel open. You do not even have to believe in yourself or your work. You have to keep yourself aware directly to the urges that motivate you. Keep the channel open.*
>
> —Martha Graham

A word about the process

Although the book asks that you proceed through each strategy in sequence, feel free to jump around. That said, your first step must involve defining your vision. You must have a vision, even if not fully developed, before you can create a mission, and you must have some understanding about your uniqueness before you can develop your mission statement.

However, the process becomes unique for each person who engages in it. As you begin to work through each stage you may feel compelled to either move ahead or go back. This is fine because your patterns of thinking and self-discovery have a journey of their own. Also, the process of discovery is somewhat like a spiral curving upward. You will revisit aspects with increased understanding and insight.

In addition to creating a mission, you will gain significant value from going through the process of developing it. The formal statement written on paper is just as important as the process of self-exploration. As stated by Plato: *The life which is unexamined is not worth living.*

In creating your mission statement you will engage in a process that involves asking questions about who you are and what difference you can make. If you have asked yourself these questions before, the answers should come more quickly this time around.

This process will guarantee two things. It will ensure that you stay on track and not duplicate steps, and it will prevent you from having to redo steps later. If for some reason you do not complete the whole book, you can return to it later and begin the process again without losing your initial learning. Indeed, each piece will fall into place over a period of time; it will not always come together at once. Do not become discouraged—this is a natural outcome of the process. As you read this book you may feel that you are on a roller coaster. You are actually on a spiral upwards as you revisit aspects of your mission from a newly enlightened perspective. Never feel as though you are repeating each time you reflect—you are looking at it differently each time.

The end product

Once you have completed the stages you should have in your hand four cards that you will review regularly. Blank cards for this purpose can be found at the back of this book. At the top of each card will be the words:

VISION	VESSEL	MISSION	GOALS
Your ideal life	What makes you unique	What you wish to accomplish	How you will achieve your mission

The content of each card will be filled in by you as you work through the chapters. At any time you can run through the stages again and refine each of the parts until your own unique picture emerges.

Synopsis

We all have dreams of being happy, but for many of us our ideals have been taken over by circumstance. This book is designed to inspire you to do what you love and provide you with the practical tools to do so. By creating a mission, you will be able to align your uniqueness with your life and work—and live your dreams.

A mission is essentially a reason for being. In its simplest form it provides direction, describes what you do, measures your success and increases a sense of well-being.

Missions are particularly important at this point in time. Baby boomers are in their middle years and beginning to ask how they can make a difference. A growing number of aging workers are seeking more heart and spirit in their lives and work, and self-employment is on the rise. These trends indicate that we are searching for our mission.

There is no best time to create a mission. Read on to find out how you can create your personal vision and bring this to fruition.

Creating Your Vision

To laugh often and much; to win the respect of intelligent
people and the affection of children; to earn the appreciation of
honest critics and endure the betrayal of false friends; to
appreciate beauty; to find the best in others; to leave the world
a bit better, whether by a healthy child, a garden patch or a
redeemed social condition; to know even one life has breathed
easier because you have lived. This is to have succeeded.
—Ralph Waldo Emerson

The first step in designing a mission is to create a vision of
where you want to be in the future. Although this sounds like a
fairly simple task, it is enormously powerful and can drive all
that you do in life and at work. Your vision is the foundation of
your mission statement and each of your goals.

A vision is the end result of what you want to have achieved
in your life. It is a picture of what your life will look like after
you have lived it. It is your ideal life. It is your personal definition of success.

The ideal vision is one that can actually be seen in your
mind. Its main purpose is to provide an ultimate goal so that
you will know where you want to end up and when you have arrived. Each person's vision will be different and entirely
unique. It will reflect all that you are and all that you want to
be. Although your vision will remain with you forever, it will
evolve and expand over time.

> *Vision without action is merely a dream.*
> *Action without vision just passes the time.*
> *Vision with action can change the world.*
>
> —Anonymous

Visions are useful in another way. In addition to providing your personal picture of success, when you adopt your vision into your consciousness, it will work toward attracting those things necessary to your success. This is called the *theory of attraction*. In essence it means that once you begin to see yourself as successful, you will begin to act as though you are successful. As a result, people will begin to act differently toward you, and circumstances will arise that support your success.

> *If you see yourself as being better you will attract to yourself those things requisite to achieving that state. You will attract all that you need. Why are some people successful and others failures? Why are some people negative while others are positive? It has to do with their vision of themselves. You cannot attract money if you have a mind-set of poverty and vice versa. Visions create order to your life.*
>
> —Bob Proctor, *Born Rich*

As you will see, one beneficial side effect of creating a vision is that much of the negative programming that we have accumulated earlier in life is replaced with a more positive perspective. Assumptions that we might have made that prevented us from being successful are substituted by attitudes of success. These assumptions are the internal programming that impacts every single thought and feeling we have and every action we take. These assumptions enable us to function. Therefore a positive vision can be enormously constructive.

In this chapter you will learn several techniques to help you create your vision as well as the specific form and components of a vision statement.

How to create your vision

Creating a vision involves creating a picture of where you will be when you are "successful." It involves using your head and your heart, contemplating as well as imagining.

Contemplating involves looking at yourself with a critical eye, asking some very candid questions and demanding honest answers. This happens at an intellectual level. *Imagining* involves dreaming about possibilities. It means letting go of all your preconceived notions about what is possible and disregarding any thoughts that might prevent you from creating an ideal future for yourself. This happens at an emotional level.

Creating a vision requires spending time alone contemplating and imagining. The ideal situation is to retreat to a quiet location for a solid couple of hours. Try to be totally free from all interruptions and distractions. This will enable you to create a completely new picture of what you want your life to look like.

It is best to select a comfortable and neutral space. If the space is too closely attached to the pressures of work or home, your creativity may be stifled. Try to limit the impact of any physical, psychological or emotional constraints. You will need some blank paper and a pen or pencil.

Creative imagination is not something reserved for the poets, the philosophers and the inventors. It enters into our every act. For imagination sets the goal "picture" which our automatic mechanism works on. We act or fail to act, not because of "will," as is so commonly believed, but because of imagination. A human being always acts and feels and performs in accordance with what he imagines to be true about himself and his environment. This is a basic and fundamental law of the mind.

—Maxwell Maltz,
Psycho-Cybernetics

In the next section I will introduce the following techniques to help you create a vision statement:

1. Define success
2. Describe your perfect life
3. Write your eulogy
4. Imagine winning a million dollars
5. Visualize future success

If you have time, try them all. The ideas that emerge through the exercises can then be translated into a formal vision statement. The final part of this chapter describes the requirements of a vision and some tips for ensuring that it is useful to you.

Method 1: Your definition of success

Although you may not realize it, we all hold in our minds a definition of what it means to be successful. We know that money and freedom are indicators of success—but what do they really mean, and how much do we need or want?

Although we all share some common ideas about success, upon deeper reflection you will discover that what success might mean to you is not what success might mean to someone else. We each value things in differing degrees. In my workshops we brainstorm what we mean by success. Hundreds of ideas surface. This is what a typical list might look like:

> The future belongs to those who believe in the beauty of their dreams.
>
> —Eleanor Roosevelt

- having freedom to do what I want;
- having sufficient money;
- being challenged at work;

- continually learning;
- having no external pressures;
- traveling six months of the year;
- having time to relax;
- meaningful friendships;
- health, fitness and energy;
- a life-long partner.

Take the time now to list the things that mean success to you. List all your needs, wants, experiences and personal qualities you wish you had. Try to turn off your internal editor for the time being. Just list everything that comes to mind. You can revise the list later.

Success means:

_____

_____

_____

_____

_____

_____

_____

_____

After completing the list, place a small heart next to the ones that you *feel* are most important. For each item you list, ask yourself *why* you want it. This will uncover deeper desires. Add these to your list.

It is sometimes easier to develop a list of what you do *not* want in your life and then translate this into positives. For example, what don't you like to do? You may not want to work ten hours a day. You may not want to commute. Rephrase these negatives as positives and add them to your list. If you are having difficulty coming up with a list, think of people who you envy or people who you think "have it all." What do they have that you want? Try to be as specific as possible.

Method 2: Your perfect life

A more concrete way to begin to think about where you want to end up is to create a picture of your perfect life—starting with your perfect day.

On the next page list all the things you want to have in a perfect day. Describe your perfect day from morning until night. Do not worry if your thoughts seem unrealistic—you are just brainstorming at this stage.

Here is an example of my perfect day:

7:00 Wake naturally and read an inspirational book in bed.

7:30 Shower slowly with special soap.

8:00 Walk to corner coffee shop and have coffee, bagel and read newspaper.

9:00 Walk to office, plan day and respond to mail.

9:30 Phone virtual assistant and delegate all administrative tasks and errands.

10:30 Alone at desk. Create, write, read and do research for books and articles.

11:30 Go for a run in the forest with a good friend.

12:00 Go for lunch with a colleague, take a break, get a massage or meditate.

1:30 Meet with clients and work on out-of-office consulting projects.

4:00 Do errands and get groceries.

5:00 Meals prepared by a chef.

6:00 Relax with wine on the deck overlooking the ocean or have guests over for a light dinner and great conversation.

10:00 Meditate and read before sleep.

Your perfect day:

7:00 _____

8:00 _____

9:00 _____

10:00 _____

11:00 _____

12:00 _____

1:00 _____

2:00 _____

3:00 _____

4:00 _____

5:00 _____

6:00 _____

7:00 _____

8:00 _____

9:00 _____

10:00 _____

Feel free to add various scenarios or alternatives for full days or for particular time slots. You may also want to keep an additional list of things to build into your schedule, such as self-development or training or leisure activities, like theatre or hikes or romantic getaways.

This exercise is primarily to help you begin to think what you really want to happen in a day and in your life. The more conscious you are of what you want, the more likely it will happen. The other advantage of this exercise is to help you appreciate how much of your current day meets your ideal day. Your vision should consist of all the things you currently enjoy.

> Many people have a wrong idea about what constitutes happiness. It is not attained through self-gratification, but through fidelity to a worthy purpose.
>
> —Helen Keller

Method 3: Your eulogy

An effective way to identify your vision is by thinking about what you want to accomplish before you die. If you live with the end in mind, you will tend to

lead a more purposeful and directed life and have fewer regrets.

Envisioning your future life can be done in a number of ways. In their book *First Things First*, Covey, Merrill and Merrill suggest that you visualize your eightieth birthday or fiftieth wedding anniversary. A wonderful celebration is being held in your honor and your friends, family and associates have been invited to celebrate you. What would you like them to say about you? What do you want to be remembered for? What difference do you want to make in their lives? Write down your thoughts here.

What I wish people would say about me:

_____

_____

_____

_____

_____

_____

Another technique is to imagine you are dead and several people are standing around your grave. Each person represents an aspect of your life and will say something about your accomplishments. What will they say? What do you want them to say? The following is an example:

- Your father might say that you were a high-energy child who always asked questions.
- Your mother might say that you were always looking out for the underdog and were a great hockey player.
- Your clients might say that you were a creative genius and also took extra time to listen.
- Your children might say you were patient and a good listener.
- Your financiers might say they could always count on you to pay back what you owed on time, and earn them a return as well.
- Your neighbor might say it was just nice knowing that you were around when they went on holiday and you loved conversing on the front lawn.

The following extract from an actual obituary might help you think about your own eulogy.

Gayman, Marjorie Alice (née Traver). Marjorie was born on March 22, 1917. She began her teaching career before World War II. Her enduring love of children, and they of her, is remembered not only in the gifts she was given each year, each with a story that she fondly recounted, but also in the special times that she brought to her children and grandchildren. She had a love of books and storytime, a love of music. Her perseverance in this area was appreciated by her two oldest children but not brought to fruition until number three. Marjorie was active in the University Women's Club and her church, to which each of her children went every Sunday, wearing clean gloves and socks. Through the Knox Ladies Club she was involved in establishing a daycare, and her passion for books led her to form one of the original "book clubs." To her regret, this in combination with the gift of reading she had instilled in her children meant that in general her books were usually in our backpacks. She was a busy mother and grandmother of five grandkids. They will always remember her for her incredible tolerance of their pranks, their sleepovers and the trips. While Alzheimer's may have affected the person we call Mona, it has in no way done anything but sharpen our memories.

A related method is to list all the things that you wish to accomplish before you die. For example you might want to:

- visit your aunt in South Africa
- skydive
- cruise in the Mediterranean
- have a baby
- sail around the world
- write a novel
- become an artist
- learn how to make sushi
- pay off your mortgage
- meet your grandchildren
- help people less fortunate than you
- become an expert in your field

After attempting the above methods, write down all the things you want to be remembered for. Try to write as quickly as you can. After exhausting all your initial thoughts, look at the list again in a more reflective way and select only those that you absolutely must have.

I want to be remembered for:

_____

_____

_____

_____

_____

Method 4: If you won a million dollars

Perhaps the easiest way to begin to think about what you really want in your vision is to imagine winning a million dollars. We all have dreams about what it would be like to be really rich. Take the time now to place your list here.

If I win a million dollars I will:

_____

_____

_____

_____

_____

_____

Method 5: Visualization

The most powerful technique for creating a vision is visualization or guided imagery. After trying this method you will be able to construct your own vision statement. Visualization is the process of using your imagination to help you uncover deeper desires and needs that may be in your subconscious mind. A kind of deliberate daydream, it involves bringing images into your consciousness. These images will alert your senses so that under the right conditions your mind and body will believe these images are real and will respond accordingly.

Visualization is a very old and powerful tool that can be used in three specific ways. It can be used to help you uncover your hidden thoughts, to imagine new ideas and to program your subconscious.

If visualization is used with guided imagery, you will be able to create pictures in your mind. These will help you identify thoughts or assumptions that might be holding you back. It will also help to clarify your ideas about what it means to be successful.

If you create a new idea — or vision — and repeat it over and over, your subconscious will eventually believe it to be true. If you place a new picture of success in the forefront of your mind, your subconscious will follow that direction.

As a result, you will attract good things to you. This is called the attraction theory. According to this theory,

> . . . the source of change and growth for an organization or an individual is to develop increased awareness of who it is, now. If we could take time to reflect together on who we are and who we would choose to become, we will be led into the territory where change originates. We will be led to explore our agreements of belonging, the principles and values we display in our behaviors, the purposes that have called us together, the worlds we've created.
>
> —Margaret Wheatly,
> *A Simpler Way*

you attract those things necessary to you and things that are moving at the same rate as you. In other words, if you think of yourself as a success, you will attract those things that are necessary to make you successful.

There are many books about the power of positive thinking and the impact of our thoughts on our physiology. Each person has enormous mind power that can be used to their advantage.

Try this: Your vision

Sit in a comfortable and quiet location. Close your eyes. Feel your surroundings. Feel your bottom in the chair and feet on the floor. Feel your breathing. Relax your body part by part, starting at the top of your head. Relax your eyes, relax your jaw, relax your shoulders, relax your stomach. What do you feel? What is the temperature of the room? What are the smells? What are the colors around you?

Imagine yourself twenty years from now. Ask yourself the following questions:

1. **Where are you living? Describe:**
   - Your city.
   - Your view.
   - Your community or neighborhood.
   - Are you inside or outside.
   - Are you near nature.

2. **What is your work or business? Describe:**
   - Your daily activities.
   - Your work setting or industry.

- Your functions and responsibilities.
- Your attire.
- Your volunteer activities.

3. Who are you with? Describe:
- Your clients.
- Your family.
- Your friends.
- Your clubs or communities.
- Your religious or spiritual group.

4. What are you good at? Describe:
- Your skills, abilities, knowledge.
- Your personal characteristics or qualities.
- Your demeanor.
- Your approach.

5. What are your leisure activities? Describe:
- Your travels.
- Your hobbies or crafts.
- Your social life.
- Your home.
- Your garden.

6. What is your lifestyle? Describe:
- Your health.
- Your fitness.
- Your stress level.
- Your weight.
- Are you smoking?

7. What do you possess? Describe:
- Your home.
- Your car.
- Your wardrobe.
- Your toys.
- Retirement savings.

Try to imagine how it might feel when you have arrived at a place you call success. The more you feel your emotions, the more precise your description can be and the more useful it will be in directing your mission and goals. After answering all of these questions, try to draw this vision here:

It is sometimes helpful to engage a mentor or coach when doing this exercise. We each hold preconceived notions about what we can and cannot accomplish and often hold mental models about ourselves that prevent us from creating a truly powerful vision. Dream big—if you don't do it for yourself, who will?

After reading about the requirements and format of a vision, you can translate this vision into a concise vision statement.

> *In the beginner's mind there are many possibilities, but in the expert's mind there are few.*
>
> —Shunryu Suzuki

Requirements of a vision

To be effective, a vision should have certain attributes. Although your vision can take many forms, the following are the main requirements of a vision statement.

Write it down

Although it can exist in your mind, it will be much more powerful if written. If you write it down, three things will happen. You will remember it, you will be able to continually expand on it and, most importantly, you will begin to integrate it into your subconscious—and begin to live it. Also, if you show it to others, you increase your commitment and will be more likely to follow through.

Put it in present tense

It must be written as if you are already there and your goals have been accomplished.

If you post your vision in a place where you will see it each day and say it out loud to yourself, it will begin to register on your subconscious. If you try to associate positive feelings with the vision, your body will begin to associate feeling good with achieving your vision. All of this translates into mind over matter, and you will begin to truly live your vision.

> *The greatest discovery of my generation is that the human being can alter his life by altering his attitudes of mind.*
>
> —William James

Provide sufficient detail

It should be detailed enough to enable you to see yourself in that specific situation.

It should be rich enough to enable you to actually feel how it feels to be there—it is not simply an academic exercise. On the other hand, your vision statement should not be so specific that you are able to pursue only one career or business. It must be broad enough to encompass the multitude of possibilities and opportunities and the many ways in which they could be realized.

Make it inspirational

Your vision should excite and motivate you. It is, after all, your ideal. It should feel just right and provide a sense of comfort and peace as well as inspiration. A vision should not add pressure to your life or make you feel as if you have to add hundreds of things to your to-do list.

Format of a vision

A vision can take several forms. Although there are no hard-and-fast rules, the following are some possible forms for a vision.

Form 1: A written definition of success

The simplest form of a vision is a written statement on a piece of paper or a 3x5 cue card. Review the answers to the exercises in this chapter. Then, on the blank card titled "Vision" that you will find at the back of this book, list all of the things that you learned.

Here is a sample vision statement:

VISION
Your ideal life
I am running or swimming every day.

I am living in a farm in the country. I own two horses.

During the day I am working at a small company with about twenty other people.

We are creating new products for new markets.

I am doing activities with my partner and children each evening.

I am healthy and eat well.

Keep your Vision card handy to ensure you are on track. You can revise it over time. I recommend keeping this card, and the other cards you will complete, in your day appointment book or wallet to review each day.

Form 2: A short biography

One very powerful form of a vision is a short biography. This is a statement that describes who you are and what you have accomplished—in your ideal state.

Biographies are used primarily for promotional purposes. You can find great biographies of authors and speakers on the back covers of popular books and in conference brochures. These are often drafted by the author or presenter and embellished by the promoter. Because of space requirements, such bios must be clear and concise, yet descriptive and enticing. I am surprised when some authors sell themselves short while others portray themselves as global experts.

The key is to draft a biography

> I shut my eyes in order to see.
>
> —Paul Gauguin

that you can grow into. The first attempt should actually make you laugh. You will probably say something like, "How am I ever going to get there?" Don't let these thoughts prevent you from writing the biography you truly wish to have achieved by the end of your life. After all, if you don't include everything you want, who will?

Another version of this exercise is to prepare the marketing materials for your business or life. Marketing experts know the precise words that will make you look like a success.

Try this: Your biography
Draft your own short biography. What does it say about your definition of success?

_____

_____

_____

_____

_____

_____

This is a sample biography:

Maureen Fitzgerald is a lawyer, author and facilitator. As an internationally recognized public speaker, she is well known for her dynamic and thought-provoking presentations. She has published several books, including

Mission Possible. As president of the Fitzgerald Group, she dedicates her time to inspiring leaders to be their best. Her bright and cozy home is in Vancouver, Canada although she travels regularly to international destinations for work and pleasure. Her daily activities include either swimming or running and she loves spending most weekends on adventures with her husband and two daughters. Maureen is continually learning and at peace.

Form 3: A painting, drawing or collage

One of the more creative forms of a vision is done through art. This includes painting, drawing or constructing a collage of photographs or pictures from magazines.

By using an artistic medium you help yourself overcome powerful thinking that prevents you from freely creating a new thing that has not existed before. Also, when you use different colors and shapes, you truly create something that is unique to you. When you look at pictures in magazines, you also begin to see what it is you might desire or how you define success. Photographs often enable you to begin to truly see how the accomplishment of your goals would actually feel, smell and taste.

Some final words

Often people do not set their initial expectations high enough. I continually urge clients to dream big or dare to dream because it takes courage and faith to believe that you can actually achieve great things. No one will dream big for you. Through the exercises in this book you will gain more courage and confidence to dream in bigger terms.

> *I always wanted to be somebody, but I guess I should have been more specific.*
>
> —Lily Tomlin

> *We cannot escape fear. We can only transform it into a companion that accompanies us on our exciting adventures . . . Take a risk a day—one small or bold stroke that will make you feel great once you have done it.*
> —Susan Jeffers

We have built-in mechanisms ensuring that we do not get our hopes too high, which can result in disappointment. These mechanisms are useful in many ways, but are the main reason we do not set big goals for ourselves. You have all seen the movie versions of the two angels that sit on either of our shoulders as we consider a decision. The white angel is the one who tells you all that is good about yourself and the black one tells you all that is bad. Although you may not realize it at the time, the black angel is usually given the majority of the speaking time. It is often easier and safer for us to simply accept the fact that we do not have the ability, the strength or the means to reach our dreams. Give your white angel more air time.

Synopsis

Visions are extremely powerful and the first step in creating your mission. Your vision is your dream or ideal state. It is your ultimate goal and forms the foundation for your mission and goals. You can begin to create your vision through a variety of techniques and specifically by answering the following questions:

- What is your definition of success?
- What does your perfect life look like?
- What do you want written in your eulogy?
- What would you do if you won a million dollars?
- How do you visualize success?

Although there are some critical requirements of a vision statement, a vision can take many forms. At the minimum it should be written in present tense, in detail and be inspiring.

In the next few chapters you will identify your uniqueness and develop your mission. As you move along you will likely want to refine your vision. For now, simply write down your vision on the card at the back of this book, read it daily and revise it when appropriate.

Identifying Your Unique Vessel

No matter what your work, let it be your own. No matter what your occupation, let what you are doing be organic. Let it be in your bones. In this way you will open the door by which the influence of heaven and earth shall stream through you.

—Ralph Waldo Emerson

In order to align yourself with your vision, you must have a fairly good idea about who you are and what motivates you. You must have an understanding of the skills and knowledge you possess as well as the attitudes you bring to your work. I call this personal description your vessel. It is the equipment that has carried you through your life so far and will continue to carry you through life. It consists of all your strengths and weaknesses and the personal tools that will help you to reach your vision.

There are three parts to your vessel: assets, approach and ambitions. When I wrote the book *Hiring, Managing and Keeping the Best*, I came to realize the following:

*A person's **assets** will tell you what that person can do, a person's **approach** will tell you how well that person can do it and a person's **ambitions** will tell you how quickly that person will do it.*

In this chapter you will begin to better understand your own assets, approach and ambitions. This understanding will help you uncover the essence of who you are and the themes that reflect the true you.

There are many career books that provide tools to help you identify your skills and interests. The career counseling industry helps millions of people each year map their particular characteristics against a job or career. Career counselors can also use psychological tests to help assess your interests and preferences.

Here you will be asked to delve a bit deeper. Although you must have a clear sense of your particular knowledge, skills and interests (what I call assets), you must also know your particular approach and your particular ambitions. This includes the special way you behave and apply what you know to situations as well as the reasons why you act. Recruiters understand the importance of approach and ambition and use it to distinguish between candidates. Once you align your vessel with your career, your positive motivation and attitude can't help but be noticed. In the assessment below, you will begin to see how unique you truly are, in ways that you likely did not consider before.

Each one of us is unique and precious. We all have talents and gifts.

> *Our first task is to discover these gifts and we shall do this by finding and following that which gives us joy. As we do so, we shall find a reservoir of energy within us and begin to create our own niche in life, our part in creation, which will be found by discovering whatever comes naturally to us. The work we were born to do leads us to find previously untapped strength of will and inner power flowing from our own spirit.*
>
> —Nick Williams
> *The Work We Were Born to Do*

How to identify your uniqueness

The following are five techniques that will help you identify your uniqueness:

- your metaphor
- your autobiography
- your childhood
- your successes
- your loves and hates

Each is described in detail below, followed by a description of how to pull them all together in terms of the three A's: assets, approach and ambitions.

Method 1: Your metaphor

A metaphor is a picture description of something. By inventing a metaphor, you create a visual and accompanying story that can be used to uncover underlying thoughts and feelings. Metaphors often disclose hidden meaning.

I use metaphors to describe the vessel that has carried you through life so far and will continue to carry you through life. It is the thing that will take you to where you want to go and will determine how you will get there. It is critical that you know what your vessel consists of and the capacity it has to take you toward your vision. This will in large part also determine your mission or the direction you will take.

Metaphors created by participants

> *Our uniqueness is our gift to the world. No two people have the same qualities, vision and experience, and our life's work emerges from our own melting pot.*
> *—Gill Edwards,*
> *Living Magically*

in my workshops include a car, elevator, shoe, roller coaster, river, hot air balloon, guitar, hang glider, skis, motorboat and seed. A popular metaphor is a tree. It starts as a small seed and continually grows throughout its life. Its branches are pruned by external circumstances. It provides shade, wood and sometimes fruit and flowers. Each tree is completely unique.

Jungle Jennifer. When I met Jennifer she saw her life as a daily fight through a jungle. She had been a public relations consultant for over ten years and told me that she wanted out. She was prepared to quit her high-paying job and work at anything to get off the treadmill that she found herself on. When I asked her to describe the jungle in more detail, she came to realize that it was not all that scary. There were very few dangerous animals, but there was adventure every day. When I asked her to describe herself, she envisioned a female Tarzan who would swoop from tree to tree helping clients and co-workers. She felt powerful at a deep level, but had gotten caught up in the tangles of the jungle. Jennifer decided to build on her known strengths, pull herself to the top of the boughs, and adopt a new perspective and approach.

Try this: Your vessel

Try to think of a vessel or other metaphor that would best describe you. What is the object that has carried you through your life? What does it look like? How does it move or function? Is it big or small? What shape are you? What color?

Draw your metaphor here:

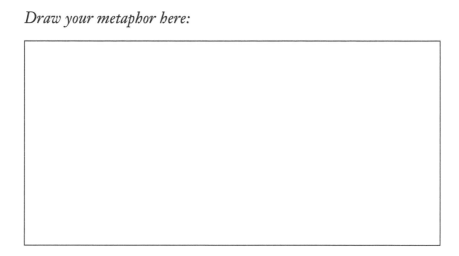

When reflecting on the above exercise, think about what your description means. Is it tired and in need of repair or is it solid and sturdy? Is it rigid or flexible? Is it capable of growth and change?

If you take time to reflect, you will uncover some hidden thoughts you have about yourself—both negative and positive. It is useful to write down these thoughts and reflect on them later. As you identify thoughts or assumptions that you hold about yourself, you will gain a better understanding of what you are capable of doing. Needless to say, it is important to uncover the strengths and weaknesses of your vessel so you can design the most effective way to achieve your vision.

You may have heard of the book called *What Color Is Your Parachute?* by Richard Bolles. Although I am not sure why he decided to use a parachute metaphor for his career book, I suspect that when he first wrote it in 1970 he thought that his book would act as a lifesaver for those who were being downsized or tossed out of their jobs. They needed a parachute to survive.

The trouble with the rat race is that even if you win, you're still a rat.
—Lily Tomlin

> *It is such a powerful feeling of fulfilling one's purpose that the experience moves to another plane. Being in the zone is the exceptional experience met in intense moments. According to those who have achieved it, it is the ultimate knowledge that you are doing what you are meant to do. The word flow itself suggests that achievement happens without struggle. You are not focussed on result, but are completely immersed in the joy of doing. Flow comes without conscious effort when you are working to your purpose.*
>
> —Lesley Bendaly,
> *Winner Instinct*

I prefer the metaphor of a rocket ship. A career transition is an opportunity to blast off in another direction to higher heights. In this book I use the metaphor of a boat, which I borrowed from the words of Kahlil Gibran in the passage *On Reason and Passion.*

A boat is a particularly powerful metaphor because it reflects life as a journey across an unknown sea. Life is portrayed as an adventure or exploration from one island to the next. During the course of our lives we each visit several islands—staying longer at some than others. Some islands are hostile, others friendly. Some may really need you; others may not like your particular style. Because of the shape of the earth you can never see the islands that are far away, so you listen to the stories of other adventurers who have been there. When you are floating between islands, you may feel as though you are adrift, being tossed around in the waves with no sense of stability. But the sun does return and the winds and smooth seas eventually lead you to a new place.

Method 2: Your autobiography

An extremely useful exercise is to draw out a map of your past. I call this a visual autobiography or lifeline. By reflecting on what you have done in your life, you will begin to recognize some common themes and identify aspects that are unique about you or your essence.

> *The events of our lives happen in a sequence in time, but it is in their significance to ourselves that they find their own order . . . the continuous thread of revelation.*
>
> —Eudora Welty

If you spend time on this exercise—perhaps adding to it over a few days—you will begin to see things that you did not see before. For example, you may start to see that much of what you have done in your life is consistent with some unique part of you. Many of your life events may now make more sense in hindsight. You may see a historical pattern or your subconscious mission statement.

One of the most interesting aspects of this exercise is recognizing how certain events lead to other events. You will quickly see how certain turning points or big decisions significantly impacted where you are today. You may even begin to look at coincidences or serendipity in a different light when looking at the whole of your life.

Dina Sampson. Dina Sampson is a forty-year-old entrepreneur. For ten years she owned and operated a tourism company on the East Coast of the United States. She started her business by finding local homes for tourists and ultimately expanded into a million-dollar full-service tourist accommodation company. A year ago she felt burnt out and decided to dissolve the company. She took a few months off to get back to the things she loved. When I met her she was keen to get into business again but had no idea what she wanted to do. She thought she could help other small business owners set up their businesses. Her visual autobiography disclosed the following:

- As a teen she worked in a park teaching children about nature;
- At university she obtained a master's degree in education and loved learning;
- For several years she lived in a cabin in Alaska;
- While operating her business she remained an active volunteer for a wildlife group;
- Her hobby is paintinge—specially bright landscapes; and
- She loves entertaining in her home.

What emerged right away was her love of nature and her desire to educate others about protecting nature. Her uniqueness was her aesthetic appreciation of nature combined with her artistic ability, the need to bring people together and the desire to educate children. A few areas of work that she began to consider were fundraising for environmental groups, writing children's nature books and designing curriculum for nature courses.

When you reflect it is critical to listen to the story that your past will tell you about who you are. What are the trends? What are the consistencies? What have you been most comfortable with over time? Your past will help you identify your core and what influenced you to take your particular journey.

Try this: Your life map
Take a piece of paper and draw a line on it from one side to the other. This line can move up and down or swirl around. Some prefer to draw a river sloping up or down or a roller coaster with high and low points. Place a zero at one end and the number eighty at the other. This represents your life expectation.

Write in your life events here:

0 __10___20 __30 __40 __50 __60__70__80

_____

_____

_____

_____

_____

_____

_____

Some of the things you will want to mark on your map are:

- education, jobs, businesses and careers;
- peak or exceptional experiences;
- leisure activities such as sports, reading and adventures;
- lifestyle activities including hobbies, arts and cultural events;
- life transitions and crises such as divorce, deaths and moves;
- people who impacted you such as friends, enemies, relatives, teachers and parents.

Be particularly alert to your emotions and specifically those times when you felt particularly happy or sad. Try to recall the voices that supported or opposed you. Look at events that emerge in combination.

Take a closer look at your particular successes. What did success mean at various points in your life? Who did it matter to? Try to identify times in your life when you were working at your absolute best. This has been called working in the flow or working in the zone.

Also look at serendipity, creative bursts, coincidences and "Aha" moments. These often do not seem so spontaneous when put into the context of your whole life. You may now be able to see why they were so important and how they often caused turning points that changed the course of your life.

It is best to take your time when doing this exercise. Keep it in a file so you can look back on it later. Each time you look at it you will see something new. *Your main task is to filter through all that you know and pull out the golden threads and themes that represent you best.* You then can weave these threads into a cloth that will form the basis of your mission statement.

Another version of this exercise is to write out a life biography in a few pages. Writing it out often causes things to surface that you might not have been consciously aware of.

Be gentle on yourself

Reflecting on your life is extremely powerful for a number of reasons, but it can have its drawbacks. There will undoubtedly be painful experiences that you might not wish to recall and there may be regrets. Rather than avoiding these events entirely, it is useful to see them as contributing to who you are today. All the events in our lives have molded us to become what we are. This is a good thing. Indeed, emotions that arise in the course of looking back are very helpful for identifying the things that most motivate or demotivate us.

When looking back, be gentle with

> *This above all: to thine own self be true,*
> *And it must follow, as night and day,*
> *Thou canst not then be false to any man.*
> —William Shakespeare

yourself. We all carry baggage that we would rather not dwell on. However, looking at the path we have worn in response to those experiences can shine a light on why we are doing what we are doing and how we got there. For example, why are you an investment banker instead of a doctor? Why did you choose the jobs and opportunities that you did? Looking at your past is just a mental journey inward. It need not be frightening or threatening.

What people said about you

When writing your autobiography it is helpful and interesting to try to remember things that people said to you at various points in your life. Often people who know you well have a particular perspective of you that is not visible to others, or to you. These people see your uniqueness. Upon reflection these comments made by others can have significant meaning.

John Andrews. The following are some of John Andrews' memories about what his mentors said to him.

- Age seventeen: A high school teacher told John that he did not have the necessary drive to go to university. He was too social and not a serious student.
- Age twenty: In John's first year of university a psychology professor pulled him aside and urged him to pursue psychology. He brushed the comments off because he thought psychology was just common sense.
- Age twenty-four: In John's fourth year of business school, a professor told him that he was very good at working with others and that he should consider a career in human resources.

- Age twenty-five: At his first job in a management consulting firm, John gravitated toward recruiting. His supervisor told him that he had a "sixth sense" in matching people to positions and had a real knack for interviewing.

From this analysis, John realized that he was always drawn to human behavior in business. He took those things he was naturally good at as being too easy. The kind of work he was drawn to came naturally and was self-motivating, rewarding and consistent with his values. John is now in human resources and focuses on executive hiring. He owns his own national recruiting company and employs twenty staff.

Method 3: Your childhood

Your childhood can tell you a lot about your uniqueness. As we experience life, we are molded by circumstances that sometimes mask what we were as children. There is a theory, called the acorn theory, which suggests that we are each born with the capacity to become all that we were meant to be. As children we did not feel the pressures of society and were more able to freely express our wants, desires and potential. Like the acorn that grows into an oak tree, if given the proper circumstances we can become what we were intended to be. Therefore, a glimpse at our childhood might uncover our true potential.

Nancy Glass worked for an international toy manufacturing company for fifteen years. After graduating from college, she accepted a marketing job for a large toy company. Within five years she had taken over responsibility for promoting and marketing a best-selling doll line.

Nancy lived in Los Angeles and traveled twice a month to international destinations. Although she loved the creative aspects of her job she came to me burnt out, saying that she wanted more control over her life. When we began to explore the things that she did as a child, one thing stood out—her love for art. Her mother had been a musician and her father was an architect who had dabbled with pencil drawings as a hobby. She collected art pieces since she was small and spent many hours searching for art and art furniture for her home. Her autobiography indicated that she had always loved decorating and that her mission was more aligned to home decoration than toys. Nancy now owns her own business manufacturing wall decorations. She loves creating and selling new ideas and concepts.

By looking at what you enjoyed as a child you will begin to see things that were of interest to you. You may have loved working with your hands, but have since abandoned this. These lost loves often point to your unique abilities and interests.

Try this: Your childhood
Think back to your childhood and teenage years. Here are some questions that can help you identify your uniqueness:

- What did you want to do when you grew up?
- What was your best sport?
- Who were your friends?
- Who were your heroes? Why?
- What was your favorite class?
- Where did you most like to go?
- What did you watch on television?

- What was your favorite game?
- Who was your favorite teacher?
- What was your favorite toy?
- Who were your enemies?
- Who did you love?
- What was your favorite food?

Write your answers here:

_____

_____

_____

_____

_____

_____

_____

When answering these questions, take the time to ponder on each. What do the answers tell you about yourself? Is there something in your current life that is related? Do you feel that you abandoned something you loved and wish you had it back?

Often the things that are unique about you are apparent at an early stage in your life. You may get a sense of security knowing that you are not all that different than you were many years ago and the things you liked then are the very things you still enjoy.

> *If our nature is permitted to guide our life, we grow healthy, fruitful and happy.*
> —Abraham Maslow

Method 4: Your successes

Your successes or accomplishments tell so much about who you are. They tell you about your skills, abilities and interests, but also about the combination of factors that make your life so unique. Although it is often easier to identify failures than successes, both types of experiences tell us about our uniqueness.

Try this: Your success inventory
List all of your successes, both work and personal, by completing the following statements:

- I was most successful when _____.
- I was at my absolute best when _____.
- I felt great when I accomplished _____.
- I felt most recognized when I _____.
- I was most happy when _____.
- I was on top of the world when I _____.
- People thought I was great when I _____.

Once you have made your list, try to explain why your successes are so important. Look behind your accomplishments. What was it that made them such big successes? Try to remember how each felt. Were you surprised by your successes? What was it about each situation that made you feel so good? What did each accomplishment represent? Are there similarities between certain events? Is there some quality or ability in you that facilitated these successes?

Here are some examples of the major successes of a few of my clients:

- learning to swim at age thirty-five;
- learning to use a word processor;

- traveling to Europe alone;
- having a baby;
- writing an article for publication;
- motivating a team;
- finishing a ten-mile run;
- making a presentation;
- buying a home;
- getting married;
- starting a new career;
- going back to school;
- starting a company.

It is sometimes helpful to have a friend or partner answer the same questions about you. They may identify other successes.

Beware of faulty perceptions

The following is an example of how one person misinterpreted her past. When looking at the past, we explain or interpret events in a way that is consistent with our beliefs and biases. This can sometimes distort reality. If you find this happening to you it is best to work with a coach.

> **Joan Bidler** is an experienced educational designer who had been fired from her last four jobs. She told me that the reason she got fired from these jobs was because her manager, in each situation, was jealous of her. Joan had several university degrees and years of international education experience. She could not find a job and felt that she could no longer work under supervision or for a boss who had fewer credentials than she did.

In my opinion, being fired from several jobs for the exact same reason would be extremely rare. Often there are many factors that determine fit in a job. I suggested that she may have constructed this perception and that it might not reflect what was really going on. We decided to look at the events again, since her perceptions were preventing her from getting a job she loved.

> *The only journey is the journey within.*
> —Rainer Maria Rilke

After a lengthy conversation, she realized that she did not have a lot of confidence in her abilities and these recent events were undermining her confidence even more. Because of this, she often accepted jobs that were too simple for her. She sold herself short when applying for jobs and often found herself seriously overqualified. As a result she saw her managers as less competent and believed (perhaps rightly) that she could do a better job. This reflection led her to adjust her perceptions that she could not work for anyone, and it helped her begin to consider jobs that were a better match for her abilities.

Two things are important here. When reflecting on your past, it is easy to see the negative, therefore try your best to look at the situation from a positive perspective. Ask yourself how an experience served you well, not how much damage it did. Also, you may be quick to find an explanation for a situation that is simply not an accurate reflection of what happened. It is best to try to look at a situation from several different perspectives. Try to find several reasons why it might have occurred. By doing this you will begin to see that there are multiple reasons and that some situations are very complex.

Method 5: Your loves and hates

One of the quickest ways to identify your uniqueness or your vessel is to reflect on what you love and hate. Very few people have the identical loves and hates.

Try this: Your loves and hates
- What do you love most?
- What do you hate most?
- What are you most interested in?
- What do you learn most easily?
- What are you talented in?
- What do you get the greatest fulfillment from?
- What comes naturally to you?
- What disturbs you?
- What frustrates you?
- What do you find difficult to learn?
- What drives you crazy?
- What is unnatural or difficult for you to do?

> *Everyone has been called for some particular work, and the desire for that work has been put in his or her heart.*
>
> —Jalaluddin Rumi

You can use this information in combination with your autobiography to begin to better understand your life journey and how it was influenced, to a large extent, by what you love and hate. For example, many of your career moves will have been motivated by a drive to move away from what you do not like to what you prefer—both personally and professionally.

The three A's: Assets, Approach and Ambitions

With the information you have elicited so far in these exercises you can now begin to translate these discoveries into your three A's: assets, approach and ambitions. Recall that your **assets** tell you what you can do, your **approach** tells you how well you can do it and your **ambitions** tell you how quickly you will do it.

You need all three to be able to fully function. Another way to look at it is: assets are your content, approach reflects the process you employ and ambitions indicate the speed or volume control. As you know, even if people have similar assets, they often differ significantly in approach and ambitions.

Assets are the knowledge, skills and abilities you possess at any particular time. You gain these from your genetic makeup, education and life experiences.

Knowledge includes what you know about the world and how it functions. It can range from knowledge about people to knowledge about science and law. It includes all the information or data stored in your head as well as your understanding of the way things work.

Skills and abilities include physical, intellectual, relationship and creative skills. Physical skills include athletic as well as technical skills, such as typing or writing. Intellectual skills involve the manipulation of knowledge, such as analytical ability. Relationship skills refer to knowing yourself and relating to others. These include communication skills and empathy. Creative skills involve such things as inventing and designing.

> *Before you can lead others, before you can help others, you have to discover yourself. If you want a creative explosion to take place, if you want the kind of performance that leads to exceptional results, you have to be willing to embark on a journey that leads to an alignment between an individual's personal values and aspirations and the values and aspirations of the company.*
>
> —Joe Jawarski

Try this: Your assets

The following is a list of skills and abilities. From the list below circle the words that relate most closely to what you discovered in the first half of this chapter.

Physical Skills

assembling	lifting	shaping
constructing	handling	inspecting
exercising	repairing	building
troubleshooting	curing	adjusting
drafting	installing	operating
renovating	aligning	moving

Intellectual Skills

synthesizing	categorizing	updating
collecting	investigating	counting
accounting	measuring	recording
sorting	classifying	sorting
auditing	manipulating	calculating
analyzing	balancing	assessing
investing	predicting	estimating
budgeting	forecasting	extrapolating
monitoring	researching	reasoning
remembering	organizing	compiling
writing	evaluating	interpreting
updating	proving	allocating
planning	diagnosing	examining
evaluating	validating	deciding

Relationship Skills

listening	empathizing	speaking
facilitating	coaching	counseling
co-ordinating	delegating	interviewing
motivating	selling	teaching
influencing	mediating	translating
advising	assisting	guiding
leading	negotiating	persuading
informing	encouraging	demonstrating
promoting	marketing	supervising
writing	serving	educating

Creative Skills

inventing	creating	designing
visualizing	illustrating	singing
drawing	painting	crafting
performing	intuiting	imagining

Your **approach** is the particular way that you make use of your assets. It is the way you do things or the *technique* you employ when solving problems or dealing with people. Your approach depends to a large extent on your personal characteristics, but is also driven to a large extent by your past experiences and influences.

Try this: Your approach
The following is a list of descriptive traits or characteristics. These will help you identify your particular approach.

> *If you do not get it from yourself, where will you go for it?*
>
> —Buddha

Review the list and circle those that best describe you. It is also insightful to have someone close to you select for you.

accurate	adaptable	agreeable
analytical	artistic	assertive
careful	cheerful	creative
curious	emotional	empowering
energetic	enterprising	enthusiastic
extroverted	flexible	humorous
imaginative	independent	inspiring
integrity	intelligent	introverted
investigative	kind	modest
objective	optimistic	organized
questioning	quick-thinking	quick-to-judge
patient	practical	productive
reflective	respectful	responsive
risk-taker	self-confident	self-directed
sensitive	shy	sociable
sophisticated	spiritual	systematic
tactful	tolerant	thorough
trustworthy	unassuming	visual

You will likely come up with a cluster of words that describe your particular approach. List those words here and revise them until they feel right to you.

_____

_____

_____

Try not to view any of your traits as good or bad, since most have positive and negative aspects. Also, be careful about the power of labels. One career book labeled all lawyers as competitive and therefore unable to work in groups!

Ambition is the motivation you have to accomplish a task or goal. Your ambitions are complex, multifaceted and personal. They are based to a significant degree on your needs, wants, interests, desires, expectations, values and attitudes.

The motives underlying your ambitions are often competing internal values that tell you that certain things are more important than others. Your motivation will be different over time and in different situations.

Motives are also affected by critical life events such as death, illness, trauma and births. When you identify this complex mix of motivation it will shine a light on the reasons why you have pursued certain things in your life.

The things you value most in life often drive your deepest ambition. For example, if you value your family relationships, then you will dedicate a significant portion of your time to this.

Try this: Your ambitions

The following is a list of motivators. Check the ones that feel most appropriate to you. What motivates you?

aesthetics	wisdom	accomplishment
achievement	adventure	well-being
affiliation	autonomy	recognition
balance	beauty	independence
belonging	challenge	financial success

community	competition	self-development
creativity	education	leading others
ethics	fairness	sustainability
variety	growth	physical fitness
helping others	security	prestige
initiative	integrity	religion
structure	learning	organization
leisure	love	nature

Reconcile this with the things you discovered about yourself earlier in this chapter. Are these the things that motivated you in your past? Do you recall being motivated by these things as a child? Did these underlie your most important successes? Are these ambitions consistent with your loves and hates?

The components of your vessel

Once you have completed the exercises in this chapter you can pull them together so that they can form your vessel. Take your answers to the exercises and write them into the following spaces.

Your assets	Your approach	Your ambitions
_____	_____	_____
_____	_____	_____
_____	_____	_____
_____	_____	_____
_____	_____	_____
_____	_____	_____
_____	_____	_____

Here are mine:

Assets
- strong thinking and problem-solving skills
- optimism and belief in each individual
- energy and excitement
- ability to write and to express complex ideas simply
- strong analytical and sorting skills

Approach
- ask lots of questions
- dislike wasting time or duplicating efforts
- take a positive solution-oriented approach
- am self-motivated and good at bringing out the best in others
- often try out new and creative approaches
- enjoy working on my own and in small groups

Ambitions
- to make the world a better place
- to facilitate learning and new insights
- to encourage breakthrough thinking
- to empower others to be their best
- to mitigate discrimination and unfairness
- to receive acknowledgment and gratitude from others
- to write in my blue jeans

The final description of who you are can take any shape or form. You may decide to keep the metaphor that you described in the first exercise, or you may create a new one. The important

Since you are like no other being ever created since the beginning of time, you are incomparable.

—Brenda Ueland

thing is that it fits you and that it describes the powerful you—the person who will carry out your mission.

Synopsis

In order to align yourself with your vision, you must know who you are and what motivates you. This includes the skills and knowledge you possess as well as the attitudes you bring to your work. I call this personal description your *vessel*. It is the equipment that will carry you through life.

There are three parts to your vessel: your assets, your approach and your ambitions. This chapter introduced the following methods as ways to begin to identify your uniqueness:

- your metaphor
- your autobiography
- your childhood
- your successes
- your loves and hates

What lies behind us and lies before us are small matters compared to what lies within us. And when we bring what is within us out into the world, miracles happen.

—Henry David Thoreau

What you discover about your uniqueness can be pulled together into a description of your vessel or your specific assets, approach and ambitions.

Before moving to the next chapter draw your metaphor and write your three A's on a 3x5 card provided at the back of this book. You can keep it with you and refer to it as you begin to develop your mission.

Developing Your Mission Statement

*The most important thing in life
is to decide what is most important.*
—Anonymous

A mission is a reason for being. It is a statement of purpose and direction and describes what you want to achieve in life and work. It provides both a beacon and a measure of success, personally and professionally.

Your mission statement flows directly from your vision and vessel. It describes how you will reach your vision in a way that is consistent with who you are. It reflects the uniqueness of you and your work.

Before beginning this section, recall your vision and vessel. If you wrote them down, pull them out and keep them handy.

The three parts of a mission statement

Each mission statement contains three fundamental components: an *action*, an *audience* or focus and an *accomplishment* or outcome. When creating your mission, the question you want to continually be asking yourself is: *What action will I take, for what people or audience and for what results or accomplishment?*

The following is the form of a mission statement:

My mission is to:

Action: _____

Audience: _____

Accomplishment: _____

The action represents what you would like to do, the audience represents the people or situation that you would like to focus on and the accomplishment is the result or outcome. For example, my mission is to inspire (action) leaders (audience) to bring about positive change (accomplishment). Although I discuss the three parts separately, they are intricately linked and should not be pinned down completely until all three parts are brought together at the end of this chapter. Often, just having the three parts together stimulates a breakthrough in thinking about your ultimate mission.

Part 1: Action

The first part of a mission statement is the action you intend to take. These actions are what you are capable of doing, what you are skilled at doing and, most important, what you want or love to do. Since most people find that they are good at the things that they love, the task of identifying your action is not so difficult. The actions that we gravitate towards are unique to each of us.

> If one advances confidently in the direction of his dreams, and endeavors to live the life which he has imagined, he will be met with success in uncommon hours.
>
> —Henry David Thoreau

The following are lists of action words or verbs. They are divided into categories that reflect *five roles* that people tend to gravitate towards: creators, builders, maintainers, provers and facilitators. The words that you select will begin to indicate the action you will take in your mission statement. You may know intuitively what cluster appeals to you or you may find you act in ways that are consistent with several groups. It does not matter at this stage—just pick the ones that feel right.

Try this: Your actions
As quickly as possible, circle all the words in the lists that feel right or move you. Go with your first impression and try not to think as you select. Choose as many as you like, then go back and reflect on the words and see how they feel.

Create	Build	Maintain	Prove	Facilitate
question	implement	operate	categorize	empathize
improvise	launch	manage	calculate	speak
dream	lift	defend	compute	listen
challenge	shape	extend	balance	promote
manifest	assemble	affirm	invest	market
reform	construct	continue	predict	mediate
invent	handle	deliver	estimate	translate
imagine	inspect	sell	collect	write
design	operate	distribute	account	negotiate
compose	program	drive	measure	persuade
devise	repair	generate	record	educate
consider	generate	organize	demonstrate	empower
reflect	renovate	serve	allocate	coach
restore	adjust	trade	measure	co-ordinate
enlighten	synthesize	entertain	analyze	counsel

inspire	draft	foster	research	mentor
discover	install	sustain	heal	motivate
visualize	acquire	integrate	compile	teach
illustrate	collect	mediate	defend	lead
generate	improve	persuade	evaluate	inspire
explore	adopt	share	interpret	involve
play	drive	understand	investigate	guide
venture	nurture	inform	diagnose	lead
love	produce	connect	examine	stimulate
encourage	engineer	command	validate	spark

From the words you circled, list the five or so that feel best:

_____

_____

_____

_____

_____

Part 2: Audience

Once you have identified the actions that feel right, you can focus on the audience or people you wish to impact. These are the people you want to help in work and life. They are your primary focus and ultimately your clients.

If you work in an organization, this audience can be either your employer or the clients of the organization. For example, an accountant for a grocery chain would focus on helping the stores in the chain record and analyze financial information. Ultimately, however, that accountant works with everyone else in the organization to provide food to people across North America. The accountant provides services to the organization and indirectly to the consumers.

You probably know a bit about your clients and can identify some of their needs, wants and interests. Ideally you should know them intimately and direct your efforts exclusively towards them. So, the more narrow your audience, the more focussed your efforts will be. Those interested in niche marketing understand this concept well and go to wherever their audience is in order to market effectively.

The people you wish to serve or impact will depend on a number of factors. The first is your current circle of contacts. For example, if you are a nurse, your current contacts consist of doctors, nurses, administrators, patients and others in the health industry. A narrower circle might be cancer nurses or perhaps women with breast cancer. There is, however, a danger in limiting yourself to this current circle. If you are heading in an entirely new direction, your mission might not be relevant to this audience.

If you work in a company, your immediate audience is your supervisor. Therefore you can think about that person as your primary audience. You can also think of the company, your co-workers, the president and the shareholders as your secondary audiences. You will quickly see how a shift in your perception about your audience can shift your thoughts about what you do and the role you play in life and at work. Keep in mind that these are your current audiences. Your future audience may be another company or many companies.

The second factor related to your audience is your past experiences and contacts. This would include people from past jobs or volunteer activities and old acquaintances.

Wayne McArdie was an investment broker who wanted to become a financial planner. His current circle consisted of some individual investors but primarily corporate clients who managed mutual funds. Two of his best friends ran their own small businesses. His past contacts included over fifty entrepreneurs that he met as a volunteer helping university graduates set up their small businesses. He was deeply concerned about retirement planning and knew that many employees were not saving enough for retirement. The audience he decided to focus on was small business owners and their employees. Ultimately he decided that his audience was entrepreneurs.

The more specific you are in defining your audience, the more likely you are to be successful. This is primarily because of your enhanced ability to focus on a particular group, but also because you will understand your clients better and will be better able to meet their needs.

Try this: Your audience
The following questions will help you begin to think about who your audience might be.

- Are they of a certain profession such as teachers, doctors, lawyers, nurses or engineers?
- Are they of a certain age such as seniors, children, teenagers, babies, or boomers?
- Are they of a certain gender?

- Do they share particular interests, such as book clubs or bird watching?
- Do they play a particular role in society, such as leaders or social activists?
- Do they share particular problems, such as being inner-city residents or survivors?
- Have they attained a certain level of education, including high school, college or university?
- Do they suffer some disadvantage, such as poverty, disability or illness?
- Do they live in a particular location, such as New York, North America or Canada?

Write down your potential audiences here:

_____

_____

_____

_____

RozeMerie Cuevas is a forty-two-year-old fashion designer who opened her first retail outlet in 1986 in a busy fashion district. RozeMerie tried to introduce some fairly progressive styles in a fairly conservative market but recalls, "No one got it. We were still in lumberman's jackets then. I sewed, I cut, I sold, I did it all. And still almost closed our doors on several occasions." In 2000, she was forced out of her location when a large retail outlet next door decided to expand into her space. RozeMerie now sees that as a blessing in disguise. Within a few months, she re-opened her shop with an intense clarity about her market. Her market is

> *I once complained to my father that I didn't seem to be able to do things the same way other people did. Dad's advice was "Margo, don't be a sheep. People hate sheep. People eat sheep."*
>
> —Margo Kaufman

busy professional women who work in the downtown core. Many have children, homes and very hectic lives with little time for shopping. Although these women are not experts in coordinating their wardrobe, they care about how they look and want a professional look. These women are value conscious and want durable, easy-care clothing. RozeMerie now operates out of her studio/store and her customers make an appointment to shop with the help of a consultant. Her goal is to make a visit to her studio a pleasurable experience so that her clients will look forward to shopping in the same way that they look forward to a haircut or lunch at a favorite restaurant.

As mentioned above, all three parts of the mission statement influence the other. As you begin to focus on the people you wish to help, you may gain a better sense of the actions you can take. In the next section, you will look at the specific way in which you can help your audience. Since all three parts of the mission statement work together, complete all three before reaching any conclusions.

Part 3: Accomplishment

Each mission statement is directed at achieving some ultimate result or accomplishment. That ultimate result is what you wish to achieve in your life or at work. It is the change or outcome you wish to bring about. It can be fairly specific or very broad.

For example, an accountant might wish to improve the way in which financial information is recorded and analyzed. This is fairly specific. Or she might wish to help the company make more profits and use her accounting expertise as one way to do this. This is fairly broad. An administrator at a local food bank might wish to improve the way that food is collected and transported to the poor. This is fairly specific. Or he might wish to create ways to prevent poverty in inner cities. This is fairly broad.

In jobs such as working for a company, or as a factory worker, even though you might not be directly helping others, indirectly you are serving society. Even though you are doing it for the sake of your salary, indirectly it does help people and you should do it with good motivation, trying to think "My work is meant to help people."

—Dalai Lama

Many people have difficulty describing what they are doing, or wish to do, in terms of ultimate outcomes or accomplishments. They can usually explain what they do now and the type of services that they provide. They can also usually identify some of the benefits their audience receives from their services, but this is just the tip of the iceberg. You must look below the surface of what you do and reflect on *why* you are doing these things. How does what you do impact your clients and others? You must ask, why am I doing what I am doing?

The following is an example of an inner conversation that leads to a mission:

- I work in a factory on an assembly line manufacturing bolts;
- these bolts are used for the wheels of cars;
- the bolts are purchased by car manufacturers;
- the cars are purchased by people around the world; and
- I am enabling mobility for people around the world.

Identifying your accomplishment: Four techniques

Uncovering the deepest reasons why you work frees you to begin thinking about the many things you could do and services you could offer. Many people, who discover their underlying accomplishments, realize that they could do several jobs. Many begin to see that their primary accomplishment is the consistent thread that underscored many of their past jobs.

> You've got to be very careful if you don't know where you are going because you might not get there.
>
> —Yogi Berra

The following four techniques will help you to define your accomplishment. They will help you articulate your passion. What triggers you? What sparks your interest? What situations break your heart?

Method 1: What is your dinner conversation?

Try to recall your last social event or the most recent dinner party you attended. Try to recall a conversation that sparked your interest.

- What was the topic?
- Why were you interested?
- Did you demonstrate your passion?
- Did you get energized or frustrated?
- Was the conversation related to the situation?
- Was it related to the speaker's attitudes?
- What was really exciting or bothering you about the conversation?

After you have worked through a particular situation, try to recall if you have had similar feelings in other situations. Try to remember those situations in detail and isolate what it was that stimulated you. Your emotional responses will often tell you a lot about what you care most about and will help you detect similarities in situations and uncover those things that you find particularly interesting or bothersome.

Write down your topics of interest here:

_____

_____

_____

_____

Madeline Oar was a CEO's executive assistant and wanted to set up a consulting practice offering personal assistance for CEOs. Her services would include dropping off laundry, gift and grocery shopping, child pick-up and other personal chores. She loved shopping and had a knack for finding bargains. She had an aesthetic sense and was skilled at putting gift baskets together.

At a recent dinner party she found herself getting worked up when the discussion moved to clutter. She felt that a cluttered work environment meant a cluttered mind. Upon reflection, she realized that she had dedicated a large part of her life to keeping other people's lives organized. She decided that her mission would be to help busy executives become organized and clutter-free.

> *Learn to get in touch with the silence within yourself and know that everything in this life has a purpose.*
> —Elisabeth Kubler-Ross

Method 2: What are you attracted to?

We are all barraged with information. Bookstores and libraries are filled with books, booklets, magazines and leaflets on thousands of different topics. Yet each of us knows or is interested in only a fraction of all that is available. What are you interested in or attracted to?

If you go into a library or bookstore, which section do you tend to gravitate towards? When you read the newspaper or watch television, what catches your attention? If you were given fifteen minutes on national television what would you want to tell the world?

Write down your areas of interest here:

_____

_____

_____

_____

_____

Method 3: What are you emotional about?

Emotions tell us a lot about what we are passionate about and care about. Unfortunately we learn at a very young age that it is not appropriate to express our emotions. As a result, they often get buried. The modern study of emotional intelligence indicates that our emotions are extremely useful at providing information that can help us become more successful.

In an attempt to identify some of your emotions, try to answer the following questions:

- When were you most happy?
- Most powerful?
- Most loved or supported?
- When did you feel most free?
- When were you most motivated?
- Most respected?
- Most at peace?
- Most angry?
- Most frustrated?
- When were you most sad?

Are there any themes that emerge? Review the questions again and try to find the things that really got you going or raised your emotional level.

Write down the themes that emerged for you:

_____

_____

_____

Real life: Reid Caper is a thirty-eight-year-old corporate forester who worked in a large forestry company for about eight years. He wanted to become a consultant. He answered the above questions in this way:
- He was most happy when he was trail running and specifically just before a big thirty-mile race.
- He felt most powerful and free when he set up his own business ten years ago selling real estate to investors. He closed it two years later.

- He felt most supported when he decided to have a family and live in Seattle.
- He was most motivated when he was presenting his ideas on changes to national forestry practices so companies could be compensated more fairly.
- Reid was most respected when he spoke up in defense of difficult issues at work.
- He was most at peace when he was at peak physical fitness.
- He was most angry when a close friend betrayed him.
- He was most frustrated with people who do not perform to their potential.

Upon reflection, Reid identified the following themes: physical fitness, continuous challenges, leading people and taking risks. He is deeply interested in continual growth, both physically and professionally. He values respect, honesty and taking risks and is passionate about bringing out the best in people and business. After doing some soul searching, he decided to accept a job as a forestry analyst, providing investors with information about forestry companies from around the world.

> *The heart has its reasons, which reason knows nothing of.*
>
> —Blaise Pascal

Method 4: What are your occupational interests?

Career counsellors sometimes use lists of careers for occupational exploration to help individuals identify their areas of interest. The following list of topics is a revised version of an occupational exploration list. If you are having difficulty identifying your particular passion, this list might help you.

Circle the things you care most about.

Art	Health	Justice	Nature
beauty	nursing	ignorance	air
nature	food	fairness	water
music	reproduction	politics	agriculture
creativity	death/birth	discrimination	trees
fashion	nutrition	equality	extinction
art	psychology	civil rights	animals
dance	spirituality	violence	biotech
theatre	safety	peace/war	plants

Mechanics	Business	Community	Educating
construction	accounting	children	facilitating
architecture	administration	homelessness	literacy
design	selling	family	broadcasting
roads	trade	sexuality	publishing
bridges	tourism	community	religion
infrastructure	technology	abused	public relations
aeronautics	management	disabled	teaching
engineering	finances	homeless	communication

Write down your main interests here:

_____

_____

_____

Another way to uncover your underlying accomplishment is to look at what you do and what you intend to do. Ask yourself why are you ultimately doing these things. As you answer keeping asking "why?" over and over, to each answer. For example, if you plan on working in a shoe shop, ask yourself why. If your answer is to provide women with more choices in color and style of shoe, ask why. If your answer is because rich women have many evening events to attend and require many different shoes, ask why. And so on and so on. Your end purpose might be to help wealthy women look great at evening events, or it may be to prevent bunions and reduce foot pain in elders. Your accomplishment is at the root of your reasons.

After completing the exercises above, insert your answers below. Read the words together and see if something comes through. You can rework your mission statement in any way you wish. It will become your first draft, which you will test in the next section.

My mission is to:

Action: _____

Audience: _____

Accomplishment: _____

Here are some examples of mission statements:

Action	Audience	Accomplishment
To help	busy executives	spend time with their families
To assist	urban children	adopt healthy eating habits
To educate	immigrants	to become more active citizens
To inspire	women	to be beautiful from the inside
To help	investors	understand the market
To assist	aboriginals	to build efficient homes
To create	artists	who can market their products

Although a mission statement must contain these three parts, it does not need to be worded as rigidly as above. You can switch the three parts around and add more content, so long as the wording does not detract from its clarity. The following are some examples of mission statements from my workshops. Although most will have likely gone through several revisions by now, the true test of a mission statement's value is its usefulness to you—the user. More on this follows.

- I help teens feel great and develop confidence.
- I provide software design solutions to small businesses.
- I reduce the frustration seniors feel when using computers.
- I provide an environment for my children to be their best.
- I assist human resource professionals deal with turnover.
- I provide technical writing solutions to large technology companies.
- I package products and information to encourage consumers to buy.
- I help babies love water and develop confidence.
- I help people with AIDS die with dignity.
- I educate children so they will respect all living things.

- I make people laugh.
- I help families travel with ease.
- I help small businesses expand internationally.
- I improve corporate work environments.
- I help organizations build respectful employee relations.

Making your mission statement useful

The value of a mission statement is in its usefulness to you and your work or business. In other words, it will be valuable if it has use and meaning for you. At the beginning of this book I described the four main benefits of a mission statement: to provide direction, to describe what you do, to measure your success and to increase well-being.

> *What moves men of genius, or rather what inspires their work, is not new ideas, but their obsession with the idea that what has already been said is still not enough.*
>
> —Eugene Dela Croix

At a minimum a mission statement must provide a sense of direction for you personally or professionally. At its best it can be used as a template for all that you do and choose not to do.

Although it has many uses, its real effectiveness is in its value to you at a very individual level. In other words, you must come up with your own individual uses for your mission statement. These uses will later be used as the criteria by which you will assess its value. The following uses or purposes of a mission statement were brainstormed at my workshops:

- To provide a beacon
- To describe what I do for a living
- To describe my business
- For promotional purposes
- As an accounting tool for myself and my business

- To provide a light at the end of the tunnel
- As part of a logo
- As a way of measuring my success
- As a way to decide what not to do
- To give me a sense of direction
- To describe my ultimate purpose in life
- To keep me on track and focussed
- To inspire, excite and motivate me
- To give me a sense of accomplishment

Try this: Uses for your mission

List here the ways in which you would like to use your mission statement. You can use this list later to assess the value and appropriateness of your mission.

_____

_____

_____

_____

_____

_____

_____

Now look at your drafted mission statement and reconcile it against the above list. For example, if you say that you want to use it to attract clients, does your draft mission statement attract clients? If not, revise it until it does.

You may end up with a few competing or inconsistent criteria, but do not worry. The ultimate test is simply whether it feels right. As you revise it over the next few weeks you will begin to sense which item feels right. You may also want to show it to friends who might help with the wording.

Keep in mind that creating your mission statement is a process that takes time. Often testing out what is not right helps to confirm what is right. By testing out the perimeters, you will be more solidly grounded in the ultimate center. Do not get discouraged.

A sample mission statement

The following is an actual corporate mission statement. Read it several times and then try to identify how it could be improved.

> *To equip professionals and managers with the knowledge, skills and information they need to identify employment opportunities and with an emphasis on obtaining and renewing business contracts as successful consultants.*

The first thing you will notice is that it is long and there are some unnecessary words. If you focus on the three necessary components of a mission statement—action, audience and accomplishment you will see the following:

> *To equip* [action] *professionals and managers* [audience] *with the knowledge, skills and information they need to identify employment opportunities and with an emphasis on obtaining and renewing business contracts as successful consultants* [accomplishment].

As you can see, the action and audience are fairly precise, but the accomplishment needs some refining. For example, what is the ultimate outcome or result that flows from the work of the organization? Are they simply educating, or are they creating successful consultants?

The real test of a mission statement relates to its usefulness to the organization or individual. Questions that need to be asked regarding the above example include the following:

- Why are we creating a mission statement?
- How will we likely use this mission statement?
- Who is our main audience?
- Who else might read it?
- How could we use it in other ways?

From this analysis you can begin to construct a more clear and concise mission statement. The following are three revised versions of the above mission statement.

Draft 1: To create successful consultants.
Draft 2: To educate prospective consultants so they can identify work opportunities.
Draft 3: To equip professionals with the tools they need to be successful consultants.

Each of these versions is a complete mission statement, but re-member that the true value comes from their usefulness to the particular user. Which of the above do you prefer? Which of these drafts meet your particular uses?

A word on values

Many people wish to add their particular values to their mission statement. This is a great way of distinguishing your services from others with different values. For example, Communicopia is a web design company that decided to focus its services on non-profit organizations that are socially and economically responsible. Their line is "Websites that matter." They became a huge success among Generation Xers who share these same values.

The following is a list of values that you might wish to include in your mission statement:

efficiency	love	learning
initiative	innovation	service
sincerity	obedience	teamwork
dependability	creativity	uniqueness
trust	community	risk-taking
excellence	loyalty	competition
freedom	environmentalism	support
wisdom	fun	candor
honesty	flexibility	originality
fairness	respect	authenticity
truth	collaboration	

Tips on drafting mission statements

The following are some tips that will help you in drafting your mission statement.

Tip 1: Do not include services or products

You will notice that a typical mission statement does not mention the specific way that the mission will be accomplished. It does not usually describe any services or products you might provide. Although you may decide to mention products or services in your mission statement, the following are some reasons not to.

If you include your services in your mission, you will be limited to providing those particular services. For example, if your mission is to educate parents about nutrition, you might not want to limit what you do to books. If you leave your mission open-ended you can continually think of new ways that might better meet your mission, such as workshops, coaching or videos.

> We will discover the nature of our own particular genius when we stop trying to conform to our own and to other people's models, learn to be ourselves, and allow our natural channel to open.
>
> —Shakti Gawain
> Creating True Prosperity

A broadly worded mission statement helps to keep your eye on the ultimate outcome as opposed to the many activities that you might do to meet your mission. As a result, it provides an excellent time management tool because you are continually thinking in terms of priorities or finding the best ways to meet your mission. It is much easier to change your services than to change your mission statement. This distinction becomes even more important when you select your goals in the next chapter.

Tip 2: Let it grow

The process of developing a mission statement is a bit like nurturing a seed in a garden. It must be planted, watered and pruned. It also needs sunshine, nourishment and time to grow. Here are some tips:

- Rework it over several months;
- Play with it and then let it rest for a while;
- Reconcile it with your past;
- Map it onto your future opportunities; and
- Read it every day to test its feel.

> *Money will come to you when you are doing the right thing.*
> —Michael Philips

Ideally your mission statement should be large enough to encompass a lifetime of careers, relationships and activities, both personally and professionally.

Tip 3: The acid test—how does it feel?

As mentioned above, the ultimate test of a mission statement is whether it works for you. In other words, does it meet the list of uses that you identified earlier in this chapter? Go back and check your draft mission against the set of criteria you developed a few pages back.

In addition to those criteria, any mission statement should be inspiring, exciting and engaging. Here is a quick "acid test" for any mission statement. If you answer yes to the following, you are on the right track.

- Does it feel right?
- Is it unique and specific to you?
- Does it reflect what you want to achieve?
- Is it exciting and motivating?
- Does it inspire you?
- Is it clear and concise?
- Is it easy to remember?
- Does it give you a sense of purpose?

Tip 4: Do not show your friends yet

When I began coaching, I told my clients that they should broadcast their mission. My intention was to help them feel its impact and also to publicly commit to it. Unfortunately, I learned that other people are not always as supportive as they could be. Some people may be jealous or suspicious of your high aspirations. Some friends may not see you in the way you see yourself. Frankly, those who do not have high expectations or confidence in themselves will not likely have much confidence in you.

> *All men should try to learn before they die what they are running from, and to and why.*
> —James Thurber

If you find that you are not supported, it is best to keep your mission to yourself until you are on a more solid foundation and can withstand criticism.

In the end, you have to decide what works best for you. Just keep in mind that most people never consciously develop a mission statement, so in most instances they will not understand what it is or why it might be useful. It is important to use common sense and make use of your mission statement in a way that will enable you to be the best you can be.

Tip 5: Keep it flexible

The entire process of developing your mission statement should be fluid and flexible. If at any time you wish to revisit or revise your vision, your vessel or your mission, you should feel free to do so.

Each stage of the process involves uncovering more about who you are and your particular uniqueness, so it is important to remain open to ideas that might come to you at different times and in different ways. Often one disclosure can lead to a series of insights about what is truly authentic about you. Remain receptive and willing to go back and reflect at any time in the process.

> *Always speak from your heart. If you speak from your heart—their hearts will hear you. If you speak from your head—their heads will hear you but they forget and grow old.*
> —Chief Dan George

Tip 6: Beware of false assumptions

The following are some of the false assumptions about mission statements:

- A mission must be spectacular;
- A mission must help a lot of people;
- Only leaders need to have a mission;
- A mission is a job description;
- Fate will determine my mission; and
- A mission must involve giving to others.

Your mission is completely yours to own. The process of developing your mission involves becoming aware of it, adjusting it so that it works for you and then living it to its fullest.

Synopsis

A mission statement describes what you want to achieve in life and work. It provides you with a purpose or direction as well as a measure of success, personally and professionally. Your mission statement flows directly from your vision and vessel.

There are three components to a mission statement: an action, an audience and an accomplishment. The action is the role you wish to play and the audience consists of the people you wish to focus on. The accomplishment is the outcome or results of your actions. By using various techniques you can begin to identify these three components. This first draft can then be tested for usefulness against your own criteria or uses of your mission statement.

Before moving on to the next chapter, write your mission statement on a 3x5 card at the back of this book.

Passion is in all great searches and necessary to all creative endeavors.

—W. Eugene Smith

STRATEGY FOUR

Selecting Your Goals and Strategies

Often people attempt to live their lives backwards: they try to have more things, or more money, in order to do more of what they want so that they will be happier. The way it actually works is the reverse. You must first be who you really are, then, do what you need to do, in order to have what you want.

—Margaret Young

Once you have created your mission statement you must begin to think about how you will accomplish it. You need to specifically figure out *how* you will bring this mission to life through action. What will you actually do? How will you do it? How will you know if you are staying on course?

To see your mission bear fruit, you must select the best way to achieve your mission, set goals and strategies, and evaluate your progress. Since there are many things that you could potentially do to fulfil your mission, you need to sort through these ideas and decide which are worth pursuing.

If you work in a corporation you must first reconcile what you are currently doing with your mission. You want to identify those things you are doing that are consistent or inconsistent with your mission. Ideally, you want most of your work to be aligned with your mission. If it is not, then you will want to either revise your mission statement or find work that is more supportive of your ambitions. This can mean delegating aspects of your job that are not suited for you, changing roles within your organization or working part-time so you can work on other more mission-related projects outside your current job. Sometimes it can mean looking for a new job or career.

If you own your own business, you must decide upon the specific products and services you will offer. From these you can set goals and strategies that translate into an organized and manageable task list.

Although many professionals focus on work or business goals, it is important to keep in mind that these goals nest within your overall life or personal goals. Your business goals are really only one aspect of your life. Your role as a professional is just one of the many roles that you play. Your other roles might be spouse, parent, friend or community member.

The following six steps will help you decide what to do, set your goals and ultimately evaluate your progress:

1. Generate ideas from your vision, vessel and mission
2. Identify your possibilities
3. Identify your internal strengths and weaknesses
4. Identify opportunities and threats in the external environment
5. Set goals and strategies
6. Evaluate your progress

Step 1: Generate ideas from your vision, vessel and mission

What you choose to do to fulfil your mission will ultimately depend on many factors, from your personal interests to the opinions of your friends and family. Therefore it is important to be systematic when deciding. The first step is to generate ideas from your vision, vessel and mission. Recall that all three are aligned. They flow into your goals.

VISION
↓
VESSEL
↓
MISSION
↓
GOALS AND STRATEGIES

Your vision, vessel and mission form the foundation for your goals. Recall that your vision is your ideal state. By providing a picture of where you want to be, you will glimpse some of the activities in which you will likely engage. Your vessel or uniqueness indicates what you are good at and what you are interested in. This provides some insight into the means you will likely employ. Finally, your mission statement describes your intended action, audience and accomplishment. These often suggest specific ways in which you could fulfil your mission.

People are always blaming circumstances for what they are. I don't believe in circumstances. The people who get on in this world are the people who get up and look for the circumstances they want, and, if they can't find them, make them.

—George Bernard Shaw

Your vision may indicate that you

are facilitating groups, your vessel may show that your strengths are in teaching and learning, and your mission may suggest that you are empowering others. This indirectly suggests that your job or services should involve educating through speaking and training.

Try this: Your activities

Look at your vision, vessel and mission statement. Do you see yourself engaging in any particular activities? List them here. Can you think of any other activities that you would like to be doing? Add them.

_____

_____

_____

_____

_____

_____

Gillian Field, is a graphic designer. Here is her vision, mission and activities.

Vision: I live in a large city near museums and art galleries. I have a wonderful husband, two grown children and two cats. I work in a high-rise overlooking the hustle and bustle of the city and work with stimulating teams of designers. I continually work on new creative projects. For a good part of my day, I am alone, drawing and creating. As an expert in my field, I am in high demand, often getting asked to join creative think tanks and idea labs. I spend one night a week dining out with friends and volunteer in my community with artistic projects and events. Each year I take several holidays to exotic locations to relax and drink great wine.

Mission: To help organizations create wonderful combinations of art and communication, provide my husband and children with a loving environment and help my community appreciate art.

Activities: My vision, vessel and mission indicate that I am doing the following activities:
- working with about five other stimulating and creative people;
- sitting at my desk in a high-rise creating bright and fantastic designs;
- problem solving with a single client on a big corporate project;
- teaching a class to college students;
- walking with a friend at noontime; and
- working with a community group on an art display.

Career professionals often have an idea about how they will achieve their mission on a professional level. For example, an accountant may know that she wants to continue being an accountant. However, she still has many ways in which she can be an accountant. Without conscious consideration, she may end up in a job that she does not like or doing things that actually work against her mission.

To compound matters, many people both inside and outside corporations take on work that does not make the best use of their skills. These jobs are often inconsistent with their interests and ambitions. Some take on too many tasks and have difficulty prioritizing. They get on a treadmill, lose focus and forget their goals. This is why a mission statement is so vital. Each day you should be able to go to work with a clear idea about your mission and goals that help you construct strategies and prioritize.

So how do you narrow down your options and focus? The answer is through strategic planning. Strategic planning consists of identifying all of your possibilities and then mapping these onto your internal strengths and weaknesses and your external opportunities and threats. These actions are covered in the following steps.

Step 2: Identify your possibilities

After you have identified some activities that you see yourself doing in the future, you are better able to consider all your possibilities. From this list of possibilities you can select those that are most appropriate for you at this time.

Your possibilities are all the different ways in which you could achieve your mission. It is the list of things you could do or the services that you could potentially provide. Take, for example, an accountant working for a grocery chain. The following are just a few of her possibilities:

Inside her organization:
- become Comptroller or CEO;
- work with management consultants in initiating change;
- create better systems; or
- train employees.

Part-time possibilities:

- create accounting software programs;
- help small businesses implement accounting solutions;
- write a best-selling book on how to make money; or
- sell accounting software and other products.

Outside her organization:

- set up a consulting practice;
- start a business offering bookkeeping services;
- set up an online accounting resource for other accountants; or
- work with management consultants in mergers.

Although you may not realize it, there are many things that you could do. You have literally hundreds of possibilities. If you look at your past jobs or your colleagues' jobs, you will begin to see the vast array of options. When it comes to being successful and achieving results, however, the situation of endless possibilities can be a problem if not dealt with systematically.

You must have an easy way to sort through your possibilities. A significant problem for some people is that they spread themselves too thin or do not have adequate focus. They end up being the proverbial "jack of all trades and master of none." Many people try to accomplish too many diverse tasks or try to satisfy everyone. To be successful, it is important to focus. In many cases this means being an expert

> *It is impossible to tell men what way they should take. For one way to serve God is through learning, another through prayer, another through fasting, and still another through eating. Everyone should carefully observe that way his heart draws him to, and then choose this way with all his strength.*
>
> —Martin Buber

in a few things or a generalist in a specific area.

If you own your own business, your possibilities are essentially all of the services and products that you could provide to your clients. Do you want to consult? Write books? Manufacture scooters? Set up a retail outlet? If you are typical, you probably have several services and products in mind. But how do you choose?

Dave Smith is the president of ExecUCoach Inc. His vision, mission and possibilities are as follows:

Vision: I live in a warm and cozy home near nature and have an office with a view of the ocean. I earn $70K a year. I work at facilitating individuals and small groups of adults to be their best. I have a few good colleagues I see on a regular basis. I take a month off each summer with my family and ski in the winter.

Mission: To help corporate executives be their best.

Possibilities:
- write books;
- write articles;
- provide workshops;
- public speaking;
- coaching one-on-one;
- facilitate small groups of executives;
- produce and sell inspirational products; or
- produce videos.

As you can see, Dave has many possibilities. He must select those that he wants to pursue and set goals and strategies for each.

Try this: Your possibilities

Think of all ways that you could potentially accomplish your mission. Write down as many as you can possibly think of, even if they seem absurd.

_____

_____

_____

_____

_____

_____

_____

You might want to expand this list by looking through job postings in the classified advertisements in your newspaper or by sharing your list with a coach or career counselor. Too often we tell ourselves that something is not possible even before we consider it. For the purposes of this exercise, it is best to be as creative as possible and try not to block any thoughts.

Step 3: Identify your internal strengths and weaknesses

Once you have listed your possibilities, you must select the ones that are most appropriate for you at this particular time. Do this by first looking at yourself and then looking at your en-

> *There is more to life than increasing its speed.*
>
> —Shatki Gawain

vironment. The objective of this exercise is to help you decide which possibilities suit you best and then map these onto the opportunities in your environment or industry.

Joan Martin is a dog lover. Her past jobs consisted of dog training and care. About a year ago she started meeting with a group of dog lovers who had recently printed and distributed a four-page newsletter to about fifty dog owners in her neighborhood. After completing my workshop, she came up with the following mission statement: *To promote the wonderful relationships that people can have with dogs.* She had several ideas about how she could do this including publishing a magazine on dogs, opening a kennel for dogs, offering seminars on how to take care of dogs and training dogs for movies. She was giddy with all of the possibilities. After looking at her strengths and weaknesses and some opportunities and threats, she decided to publish a pet magazine and continue training in her spare time.

Your strengths and weaknesses are your own internal advantages and disadvantages. Your unique vessel describes many of these. Look at your vessel cue card and list your assets, approach and ambitions here. These should reflect most of your strengths.

Your assets: _____

_____

_____

Your approach: _____

_____

_____

Your ambitions: _____

_____

_____

You can expand on these now if you see other strengths that were not identified earlier.

_____

_____

_____

_____

_____

_____

Your weaknesses are simply the flip side of your strengths and can be thought of in the same way—as negative assets, approach and ambitions. For example, what assets or skills are you lacking? What approach or techniques do you need to improve? In what ways are you demotivated?

Your weakest assets: _____

_____

_____

Your weakest approach: _____

_____

_____

Your weakest ambitions: _____

_____

_____

When reflecting on these weaknesses you need to think about two things: Are they necessary to your success and if so, how will you overcome or compensate for them? No one is competent in everything—but if competence is required, you should begin to think about ways to achieve it or find others who can fill this gap.

Step 4: Identify opportunities and threats in the external environment

Opportunities and threats are those things that impact you from the outside. They exist in the environment in which you work as well as the larger market.

One way to identify opportunities and threats is by reading about trends. There are several books published each year that look at major trends in the world and in specific markets. You can also learn by reading magazines and newspapers and speaking to others in your industry. This market research should be done on a continuous basis, even if you are working within an organization.

One of the main trends affecting North America is the effect of the baby-boom generation and their

It's a funny thing about life; if you refuse to accept anything but the best, you very often get it.
—Somerset Maugham

consumption habits. More specific trends can be caused by policy or spending changes by corporations or governments. When corporate or government programs are cut or underfunded, there is an increased demand for these services from new sources. For example, funding cuts to hospitals will result in an increase in private health services.

Take a moment now to list the opportunities and threats that you know about that have some relation to what you want to do. After researching your market you can expand on these.

Opportunities: _____

_____

_____

Threats: _____

_____

_____

As a business owner, you should be engaging in this process on a continual basis. You must always keep an eye on your competition and be able to respond to market shifts.

The possibilities grid

Once you have identified your possibilities, strengths, weaknesses, opportunities and threats, you can fill in a grid like the following. This is a tool that will help you sort through your opportunities and select the best way to achieve your mission. If you are in business, it will help you select the specific services and products that you should offer. A partially completed grid for Dave Smith follows. A larger blank grid can be found at the end of this chapter.

Possibilities	Strengths	Weaknesses	Opportunities	Threats

Dave Smith and ExecUCoach Inc.

Possibilities	Strengths	Weaknesses	Opportunities	Threats
Write books	Writing comes naturally to me.	I am a perfectionist so I can spend an inordinate amount of time writing a chapter.	Sales of books on the topics I write are on the increase.	There are several competing books.

Possibilities	Strengths	Weaknesses	Opportunities	Threats
Write articles	I like writing and reaching large audiences.	I am not great at summarizing my thoughts into smaller articles.	Magazines in general are always in need of articles.	Few magazines cater to my specific industry.
Provide workshops	I love to inspire clients face to face. I am consistently rated as an excellent trainer in every session I conduct.	I am not a great facilitator and design takes time. I have a limited budget to rent training space.	New executive offices are popping up for training space. There are many teachers looking to help with training. People are paying more for tailored training.	Time-consuming and costly to promote. Market is saturated with similar offerings and it will be difficult to differentiate my product while maintaining my price.
Public speaking	My message could reach lots of people. I am charismatic and funny.	I am intimidated by large groups of people.	There are many different venues to offer public speaking and it is not limited by location.	Demand is sporadic for public speakers.
Coaching	I love it and it is powerful for clients. I am a great listener and empathetic.	My tendency is to want to give advice and move quickly. I need to remind myself to be more patient and let the person move at a speed that is comfortable for them.	Executives and managers are more readily seeking out coaches to help them become more successful (trend).	Competitors include psychologists, counselors and consultants.

> *Do what you love. Do what makes your heart sing. And never do it for the money. Don't go to work to make money, go to spread joy.*
> —Marianne Williamson

As you probably realize, one of the disadvantages with this exercise is that it is entirely subjective. All of the information that you place in the grid reflects your opinion, based on your own experiences. Since these are, at best, educated guesses, they should be tested in some way. The easiest way to do this is by seeking the help of an objective outsider. This could be a colleague or business coach, someone in your industry or a trusted friend. Also, look back at all of the feedback others have given you over the years—at work and personally.

Try to be honest and realistic in your answers, but not too negative. If you are having a difficult time, take a break and come back to it later.

This grid can be an extremely handy tool to keep and build upon. As you get busy at work, periodically stop and ask yourself, is this one of my strengths or weaknesses? Is this work an area in which I wish to grow or one to abandon? Now that you understand better what you must be alert to, you can begin to see opportunities and threats in ways that you might not have before. In a few months come back to this grid and you will be surprised at how much you have learned about yourself and your environment. Go through the exercise again and refine your grid.

Step 5: Set goals and strategies

By completing the possibilities grid you will begin to get a clearer idea about what you want to do. The specific activities you select become your portfolio and from this portfolio flow your goals.

Here is a sample portfolio and possible goals:

Portfolio	Possible goals
Coaching	Provide coaching to twenty executives.
Provide workshops	Teach three workshops on coaching.
Group coaching	Conduct three group coaching sessions.
Public speaking	Speak at three large group events.
Write articles	Write two articles for business magazines.

Ideally your goals should be SMART: specific, measurable, achievable, realistic and timed. For example, if you want to provide workshops, you should specify what they will be about, who they will be for, when they will be held and how much they will cost. However, some prefer to write more generic goals and add the specifics when they sort out their strategies. This will become clearer later when you design strategies and set priorities.

An ideal set of goals will include both long-term and short-term goals. For example, a ten-year goal might be to sell the whole business at a profit, while an annual goal might be a specific profit level. It is very important to look further ahead than just a few months or years. It is ideal to set goals at ten years, five years, one year, six months and three months, and review your goals every three months to ensure you are on track.

Different types of goals

Although the focus so far has been on your professional side, you should also include your financial and personal sides when setting goals. Professional goals relate to your development as a professional at work. Financial goals are essentially the financial targets you set for yourself and your business. Personal goals relate to your health and personal relationships. Fully developed missions will include personal, professional and financial aspects and thus the goals should reflect this.

If you own your own business you will also have corporate goals. These relate to your organization as a separate entity and have to do with such things as finances, structure, marketing and research and development.

Here are two examples of missions and goals.

Gillian Field is the graphic designer you met earlier in this chapter. Her mission and goals are as follows:

Mission: To help organizations create wonderful combinations of art and communication, provide my husband and children with a loving environment and help my community appreciate art.

Personal goals:
- to keep healthy and fit;
- to raise my children to be loving and respectful;
- to support and nurture my husband and his career; and
- to play an active role in the arts community.

Professional goals:
- to provide design services to my current corporation;
- to contribute as a team member in my department;
- to establish myself as an expert graphic designer;
- to keep skilled and up-to-date; and
- to educate others about the value of graphic design.

Financial goals:
- to earn $80K net a year.

Dave Smith is the president of ExecUCoach Inc. you met earlier in this chapter. His vision, mission and goals are as follows:

Vision: I live in a warm and cozy home near nature and have an office with a view of the ocean. I earn $70K a year. I work at facilitating individuals and small groups of adults to be their best. I have a few good colleagues I see on a regular basis. I take a month off each summer with my family and ski in the winter.

Mission: To help corporate executives be their best.

Personal goals:
- to get married;
- to cat better and lose ten pounds;
- to get into a regular exercise regime; and
- to spend more time with my family.

Professional goals:
- to provide one-on-one coaching to twenty executives;
- to teach three workshops on coaching;
- to conduct three group-coaching sessions; and
- to speak at three large group events.

Financial goals:
- to earn $70K net a year.

Corporate goals:
- to become incorporated;
- to network and tell others what I do; and
- to keep informed and skilled.

Strategies and priorities

Once you have defined your goals you can then develop strategies and set priorities. Although this may seem like a science, it is very much an art. What you might describe as a goal may be another person's strategy and vice versa. The objective of this exercise is to translate your largest goals into bite-sized chunks so that you can prioritize and manage them more effectively.

The following are the goals from above with an additional column describing examples of strategies. Ideally each of your goals and strategies should comply with the SMART rule. They should be specific, measurable, appropriate, relevant and timed.

Dave Smith's goals and strategies

Personal goals	Strategies
Get married.	Join a dating service by next week.
Eat better and lose ten pounds.	Hire a nutritional consultant by June.
Get into a regular exercise regime.	Buy running shoes and run three times a week at noon, starting next week.
Spend more time with my family.	Call my parents once a week.

Professional goals	Strategies
Provide one-on-one coaching to twenty executives.	Meet with ten colleagues who are "influencers" over the next four months.
	Join an executive club by March.
	Offer two lunch and learns by September.
	Contact twenty CEOs directly over the next six months.

Professional goals	Strategies (cont'd)
Teach three workshops on coaching.	Research those who teach about coaching by February. Locate and meet three other facilitators before May. Design a course for local college before June. Offer a public workshop by August.
Conduct three group-coaching sessions.	Research who does group coaching in April. Join a coach group in February. Offer a group coaching session to career consultants by March.
Speak at three large group events.	Research speaking opportunities by February. Send in proposals for three relevant conferences by March. Offer to give free talks to groups of more than thirty people to ten companies.

Financial goals	Strategies
Earn $70K net.	Prepare a budget by the end of January. Create a fee schedule by the end of January. Set up accounting system by the end of March.

Corporate goals	Strategies
Become incorporated.	Fulfil government requirements by January 30. Create business cards and stationery by February. Lease or purchase office equipment, as needed.

Corporate goals	Strategies
Network and tell others what I do.	Design and mail promo card to all friends and colleagues by February. Follow up with meetings: two a week for the first six months. Write two articles in local media in February and July.
Keep informed and skilled.	Read about trends regularly. Subscribe to local business newspaper by March. Join relevant discussion groups by April. Surf Internet regularly. Join related professional groups by June.

Step 6: Evaluate your progress

The final step after setting your goals and strategies is to evaluate your progress. This will ensure you keep on track. Review your vision, mission, vessel, goals and strategies every few months and walk through the strategic planning steps again. This is a good time to bring in a mentor or coach who will question your assumptions and help you create new ideas for moving ahead.

> *If you always do what you have always done, you will always get what you have always gotten.*
>
> —Anonymous

Synopsis

Once you have your mission statement, you must decide how you will achieve that mission. Since there are many things that you could potentially do to fulfil your mission, you need to sort through all of your possibilities and decide which are worth pursuing.

Whether you work within a corporation or on your own, you must consciously select the work you will do or the services you want to provide. At the minimum your decision-making process must be systematic. I recommend the following steps:

1. Generate ideas from your vision, vessel and mission
2. Identify your possibilities
3. Identify your internal strengths and weaknesses
4. Identify opportunities and threats in the external environment
5. Set goals and strategies
6. Evaluate your progress

You should now have a clear idea about how you will accomplish your mission. You should have a list of goals and strategies and be ready to implement your mission into your life and work. Before starting the next chapter, write your goals on the 3x5 cue card provided at the back of the book.

Possibilities Grid Worksheet

Possibilities	Strengths	Weaknesses	Opportunities	Threats

Taking Action

We have stifled our natural self and our spirit through the conditioning that we have absorbed throughout our lives. Our conditioning is the beliefs, attitudes and opinions that others have invited us to take on, which we may have mistaken as facts.

—Nick Williams, *The Work We Were Born to Do*

Even if you have a well-designed mission statement there is a possibility that it will not come to fruition. There are many reasons why your mission might fail. Some reasons are internal and some are external. You may not possess the necessary abilities or attitudes, or you may not have the necessary resources. Some problems are within your control while others are not.

This chapter introduces five strategies to help ensure that your mission becomes a reality. Armed with your vision, mission and a clear description of what you want to do, you are ready to take action. This means going out into the world and dealing with all the opportunities and challenges that come your way. I recommend the following five strategies

1. Integrate your vision and mission
2. Identify your supports
3. Adopt appropriate attitudes
4. Face your fears
5. Stay focussed

Strategy 1: Integrate your vision and mission

The power of your vision and mission depends upon the extent to which you integrate them into your life. It is not enough to simply think about them and then forget them a few days later. You must write them down, read them regularly, and truly live them.

If used appropriately, they will become like second nature and you will no longer have to think about them. When someone asks you to describe what you do, you will be able to clearly state what your mission is and name the specific means by which you are accomplishing this mission. You will be directed by a clear set of goals and priorities and know with certainty that you are living and working in a way that is consistent with your uniqueness. You will be able to screen new opportunities against your mission and confidently accept those that are consistent with your mission or, conversely, reject those that are inconsistent.

The only way to get the full benefit of your mission and vision is to truly integrate them into your life.

Strategy 2: Identify your supports

Although you might often feel that you are alone, you are not. The truth is that you are surrounded by people and resources that can be both positive and negative. One of your first goals should be to identify those people and resources that will support you in life and at work. You may not have realized it, but there are many people waiting to be called upon and who are happy to give their support.

Fall seven times, stand up eight.

—Japanese proverb

The first group of people you should turn to is your *friends and colleagues*. They are often curious about what you are doing, and each one of them has their own circle of friends and colleagues who might be interested in you or your ideas.

> *Keep away from people who try to belittle your ambitions. Small people always do that, but the really great make you feel that you too can become great.*
>
> —Mark Twain

The next group of people you should turn to are those who are in your industry who are potential *collaborators*. Many share your concerns and are genuinely interested in what you are doing. They want to know what is new and like to associate themselves with people like themselves. These contacts often lead to job offers and referrals.

If you have your own business, you might also want to speak to your *competitors*. Although this might sound odd, many of your competitors are not able to do all the work that comes their way. They may be too busy or in a conflict of interest. Often clients seeking help want to select between two or more companies. They will sometimes ask for the names of others so they can compare services.

Whether you are inside or outside a corporation, it is critical to keep other people informed about what you do. Part of this can be accomplished by staying in touch with your colleagues, collaborators and competitors. The market for your services and products continually changes and so must you. You must anticipate what is happening and adjust accordingly.

When identifying supports, you will undoubtedly come across people who do not support you. This includes those who might be interested in taking your job or your business away. Some might be afraid of your success and how it might reflect on them; others simply do not support you, for whatever reason. In the same way that you search out supports, you must be constantly aware of threats.

> *Your beliefs are your reality. Beliefs are assumptions about the nature of reality, and because you create what you believe in, you will have many "proofs" that reality operates the way you think it does.*
>
> —Sanaya Roman, *Creating Money*

Jake O'Leary, a young lawyer, recently spoke to me about his difficulty in securing a new job. He decided that he wanted to combine his interests in sports and law. Several lawyers Jake had spoken to had told him that almost every male athlete lawyer they knew wanted to be sports lawyer. During coaching I suggested he stick to his vision and mission and speak to as many people as possible about sports law. We agreed that it would be best to avoid those who recount stories of doom and gloom and search for those who support his dream. He decided to ask each person he met for the names of three others who might be able to help and send a note of thanks after each meeting. He would maintain a list of those who supported him and keep them up to speed on his progress.

Many people will not support you, and many will either consciously or unconsciously undermine you. Some may even persuade you to fail. These people may be kind-hearted and trying to protect you from making a mistake or getting your hopes up. They may not realize that getting your hopes up is critical to your success. Some fail to see your assets, approach and ambitions, while others may care about you but just not be interested in your success or failure. The ideal is to surround yourself with people who bring out the best in you. People who support and challenge you enable you to extend yourself beyond your own mission.

Strategy 3: Adopt appropriate attitudes

Your existing beliefs have a powerful effect on your life. From the day that you were born, you began to make sense of the world and attribute meaning to the things that happened around you. In doing so, you created a personal system of meaning that includes thousands of assumptions, attitudes and opinions about what is happening and what might happen in each situation. This process of learning fundamental beliefs is often called *conditioning*.

Most of our assumptions are necessary to our survival and day-to-day living. For example, we assume that a green traffic light means Go and a red light means Stop. We learn that certain behaviors are appropriate and others are inappropriate. These personal systems represent what is possible for us personally.

Everything we do and feel is based upon this constructed perception of the world. Each new experience is filtered through these frames of reference or mental models—often distorting what is really occurring. Simply put, whatever you believe to be true is true! Your beliefs control your future. Your beliefs tell you what choices you have. They are critically important.

Two potential problems can arise from your conditioning. First, your perceptions and attitudes may not be grounded in reality and may be preventing you from getting what you want, and second, the conditioning may be hiding your true self.

Many years ago, Francis Crick, winner of the Nobel Prize for his work on DNA, was asked why only a few scientists made valuable discoveries. After reflecting for a moment, Professor Crick said that the most important

> *Water originally contains no sound: Touching a stone makes it murmur.*
>
> —Zen saying

reason was because people were handicapped by assumptions that they were not even aware that they were making.

> Be selective when choosing new friends and associates. Is this person someone you want in your life for years? Do you share similar values and interests? Does this person know how to be a friend? Choosing relationships is like buying the correct ingredients for a special meal. You might be an excellent cook and have a great recipe, but if your ingredients are not appropriate, the meal will not turn out. So it is in life. You can have a good recipe for success—high potential and a clear soul's purpose—but if you choose friends and work associates that do not enhance that purpose, even though they might be wonderful people, you may become distracted from your goal.
>
> —Tanis Helliwell,
> *Take Your Soul to Work*

Most of our beliefs originate in childhood. Often these are reinforced by the community in which we live. For example, some religions promote the belief that we are being punished for some former wrong. If we live a hard life, when we die we will go to heaven to live in an endless state of joy. If you subscribe to this belief, you will not likely aim for a life of comfort and happiness.

All of the learning that results from our life experiences conditions us so that we behave in a way that is consistent with these beliefs. Indeed, the most powerful learning is through painful experiences. These experiences often register with our body at such a deep level that they become subconscious and beyond our awareness. They sometimes manifest themselves as unexplained fears.

The three R's: Recognize, reflect and refine

In order to deal with negative attitudes or fears you must recognize them, reflect on them, and then refine them so that they can begin to work for you and not against you. In other words, you must recognize what is going on in your inner mind and challenge it. You must then sort out your beliefs and attitudes and consciously reinforce those that are constructive and healthy and abandon those that are destructive or unhealthy.

It is important, therefore, to understand that circumstances in our lives actually have no power over us in and of themselves. We give them power through our thoughts. Our attitudes and fears can be altered and controlled through our thoughts. We have the power to control and change our thoughts and behaviors.

When looking at your own personal attitudes, three specific areas are important to explore. The first relates to how you perceive *yourself*, the second relates to how you relate to *money and power*, and the third relates to your perception of *success*. Attitudes relating to each of these areas originate from your own personal experiences and must be recognized, reflected upon and refined. Otherwise, they can prevent you from becoming a success and fulfilling your mission.

1. Attitudes about yourself

One of the main reasons why people do not follow their mission is because

> Isn't it a strange idea that we have made of God, who would create us with love, creativity, passion, inspiration, beauty and joy woven into our being and then demand that we spend the greatest part of our lives—work—totally discounting, hiding or ignoring all these gifts? We create a picture of a God who thrives and flourishes on our suffering. Somewhere we've misled ourselves, and overlooked the fact that life is set up to support us doing what we enjoy, following our heart's desires and being where our passion is. The opposite of sacrifice is not hedonism, but authenticity and truthfulness.
>
> —Nick Williams,
> The Work We Were
> Born To Do

of a lack of self-esteem. They do not believe that they can be successful doing what they love.

Most people are held captive by programming about what success means to their parents or society. Many people are unhappy in their careers and are working at unsuitable jobs because they are trying to fulfil someone else's dream, instead of their own. Self-esteem is critical to success.

Although self-esteem develops over a lifetime and there are particular ways to enhance it. The best way to develop self-esteem is by doing something well and feeling good about it. Self-esteem evolves from consistently succeeding. However, because our self-esteem is so deeply embedded in our being, we are often not able to see that it is preventing us from succeeding or that it is changeable. It becomes like a shadow we carry around that prevents us from doing great things.

To help you recognize your level of self-esteem, ask yourself the following questions:

- Do you believe in yourself?
- Do you believe you have the capacity within you to fulfill your wishes?
- Do you believe you can earn money doing what you love?
- Do you think you have the strength to succeed?
- Do you feel you are unique?
- Do you think you have control over your life?
- Do you believe you are a victim of circumstance?

One way to improve your self-esteem is to improve how you think about yourself. You can do this in two ways, and you should do both. First, start doing what you love and keep succeeding, and second, learn to critique your negative thoughts and replace them with positive thoughts.

You must believe you are fundamentally good inside and that change and opportunity come from inside you. Your success does not depend on the perspectives that others have of you. You must put aside the belief that you are a victim of circumstance and that everything good is outside of you. You must believe that you are unconditionally lovable. You are complete and whole and continually growing. Your power comes from you and no one else. Think of the alternative. You must believe in yourself. If you don't, who will?

2. Attitudes about money and power

Each of us has a collection of attitudes about money and power—some positive and some negative. If you have negative thoughts about money and power you must recognize them, reflect on them, and refine them so that they support you. The following list of sayings will help you begin to uncover some of your hidden thoughts about money:

- Money is the root of all evil.
- Money is hard to come by.
- Money does not grow on trees.
- You can never have enough money.
- Save your money for a rainy day.
- A penny saved is a penny earned.
- Be grateful for what you have.

You may have heard your parents' voices as you read through this list. This is because many of these thoughts were imprinted on us at a very young age. Unfortunately they prevent us from making more money. We subconsciously push money away or limit our moneymaking potential.

Recall some thoughts you might be harboring about money here:

_____

_____

_____

_____

_____

_____

After you have completed this list, think of positive phrases to replace them.

These are just a few of the hidden thoughts that direct the way you behave. Your task is to identify those that do not support you and get rid of them.

Most people would readily admit that money is necessary, indeed critical, to most definitions of success. Money enables us to do the things we want to do. It gives us choice and freedom. Why then do we think that money is bad? Where do these assumptions come from? Are they based on reality? How does that reality relate to our lives?

If you want money, you must value it. This means believing that it is not just useful, but good and wonderful. You must try to rid yourself of the negative connotations that you attach to money or you will subconsciously be rejecting it.

In her book on personal power *Creating True Prosperity*, Shakti Gawain urges individuals to uncover their subconscious attitudes about power and to abandon those that prevent them from becoming powerful. She urges us to think of power in a more positive light. Here are some of the questions she asks the reader to reflect on:

- If I get too powerful I might . . .
- My mother/father thinks power is . . .
- Powerful people are . . .
- Power is dangerous because . . .
- A powerful woman is . . .
- A powerful man is . . .
- The advantage of not being powerful is . . .
- If I were powerful I would . . .

What does having power mean to you? Does it mean something positive or negative? Would you feel bad if you had more power or money than others? Are you subconsciously sabotaging yourself? Can you trust yourself to use money and power wisely?

Write your attitudes about power here:

_____

_____

_____

_____

_____

_____

Once you have identified some of your attitudes about money and power, you will want to refine them or replace them with more appropriate attitudes. The following list of thoughts can replace some of your negative thoughts about money and power:

- Money is wonderful.
- Money can buy me freedom to do the things I love.
- Power is a good thing.
- Power means the ability to accomplish or influence things.
- Power does not mean control over others.
- Personal power enables others to be empowered.

3. Attitudes about success

Although you may sincerely want to be happy and successful, your subconscious may think otherwise. You may have hidden attitudes that success will bring bad things, a deep belief that you are not deserving, and a perception that there is not enough to go around. Each of these three attitudes must be addressed.

Often the idea of being extraordinarily successful makes people feel uncomfortable. It may be too overwhelming or it might seem like too much responsibility. Because you may not be aware of your attitudes, try to put yourself in a position of success. Ask yourself: What if I am a huge success? Does your answer look like this?

- I will be too busy and stressed.
- I will be working all the time.
- I will have to hire people to help me.
- I will not be able to respond to client needs and will fail.
- I will not be able to spend time with my family.
- I will have to sacrifice something.

- I will be all alone.
- I will become selfish and competitive.

These attitudes may be subconsciously preventing you from being successful. Recall that when you created your vision earlier in this book, you developed your own definition of success. That definition probably looks like the exact opposite of your list here. In other words, if you want to be successful, you can't think like this.

Write down a few of your own attitudes about success here:

_____

_____

_____

_____

_____

_____

Sometimes our attitudes about success are related to a sense of not deserving a good life or a sense of guilt for being too successful. You may have been raised to believe that you only get what you deserve and that to deserve anything you must work very hard. You may have learned that you must give up something in exchange for happiness or a successful career. Unfortunately, these thoughts prevent you from being all that you can be.

> The strongest single factor in prosperity consciousness is self-esteem: believing you can do it, believing you deserve it, believing you will get it.
> —Jerry Gillies, *Money Love*

Try answering the following questions to help identify whether you truly think you are deserving:

- Do you think you deserve to be successful?
- Do you think that life must be painful?
- Do you think that people who are successful deserve to be so?
- Would you feel guilty or apologetic if you were really rich?
- Do you believe you can make money doing what you love?
- Do you think you can't always get what you want?
- Do you think you can have your cake and eat it too?

A more constructive perspective is to believe that you are deserving just because you are alive. You already are a success. Write down a few notes about your current negative attitudes and think about an attitude that might be more positive.

Current attitudes	New positive attitudes
_____	_____
_____	_____
_____	_____
_____	_____
_____	_____
_____	_____

The third type of attitude about success relates to a sense of scarcity. This is a belief that there is not enough to go around. Many of us were raised to believe that the world is an endless competition for a finite amount of resources—food, money, opportunities and even love. If you think this way, your odds of succeeding are very low. This attitude causes us to move into a position of defense. It causes fear and cripples our ability to take reasonable risks. Because it is so easy to focus on the negative, as opposed to the positive, many people tend to look at what they do not have or what is missing from their lives as opposed to what they do have.

If you believe the following, you have an attitude of scarcity:

Alpha women may not be who you think they are.

They are astonishingly energetic, and have a gift for taking charge and getting things done. But they are not driven by a desire for power or a need to dominate others, but by clarity of vision, resoluteness of purpose and a delight in accomplishment. Their need to govern does not apply to people but to circumstances.

—Anne Giardini

- There is not enough to go around.
- My luck won't last.
- My win is another's loss.
- I will never be able to earn enough money.
- There is too much competition.
- There are no new ideas.
- There are no jobs for me.
- Why would anyone hire me?

Once you have identified your negative attitudes, you must refine them or replace them with more appropriate ones. In other words, you must believe that being successful will bring you happiness, that you deserve to be successful and that there is lots to go around. List a few attitudes you have about scarcity or lack of abundance and a few new attitudes to replace the old ones.

Current attitudes	New positive attitudes
_____	_____
_____	_____
_____	_____
_____	_____
_____	_____
_____	_____

When it comes to success it helps to adopt an *attitude of abundance*. This means believing that there is more than enough for everyone. The following are thoughts that flow from an attitude of abundance:

- There is lots to go around.
- I can do many different things well.
- Everyone has many gifts and talents.
- I have skills to fill a particular niche.
- Others benefit by me living authentically.
- I can attract the things I need to succeed.
- The world if full of opportunities.
- I have the power to fulfil my dreams.
- I deserve to be successful.

Strategy 4: Face your fears

Fears, like attitudes, exist in our minds and can be either healthy or unhealthy. Some ensure our survival, while others prevent us from becoming the best we can be. Fears protect us in a very instinctual way from dangers—either real or perceived. Fear is the feeling we get that tells us that danger is near and we must be cautious. Our ability to detect and re-

spond to fear is necessary and geneti-
cally hard-wired.

The main problem with fears is that,
in many situations, they prevent you
from doing something that is beneficial. They limit your risk-taking behavior and can prevent you from
becoming successful.

In order to face your fears it is
helpful to recognize where they originate. Some fears are carried from
birth, but most are developed
throughout our life through our own
life experiences. Many of our fears
are based on a *perception* of danger.
The following are examples of some
shared human dangers and our related underlying fears:

> *Scarcity mentality is the root cause of most fear. This mentality is characterized by such thoughts as, "There's not enough love, success, money, happiness for everyone." This thought leads naturally to the next one, "There are winners and there are losers." In making that connection, we put ourselves into one of those two categories, based on our self-esteem and life experience.*
>
> *—Tanis Helliwell, Take Your Soul to Work*

Danger	Sample fear
Physical danger	You will not have the strength or energy to survive.
Psychological danger	You will not have the willpower or courage to succeed.
Social danger	You will be rejected or ruin your reputation.
Intellectual danger	You will feel stupid or be outsmarted.
Economic danger	You will go broke or starve.
Spiritual danger	You will become self-centered and be alone.

In *Think and Grow Rich*, Napoleon Hill identified the following six fears:

- fear of poverty;
- fear of criticism;
- fear of ill health;
- fear of loss of love;
- fear of old age; and
- fear of death.

Fears can emerge slowly over time and are often hidden. Unless you place yourself in dangerous situations on a regular basis, you may not even know that you are afraid or are avoiding fearful situations.

> *Success is the ability to go from one failure to another with no loss of enthusiasm.*
> —Sir Winston Churchill

Although fears will come and go as a natural consequence of certain activities, it is useful to develop a better understanding of your deeper fears. This enables you to develop better ways to deal with them when they do arise. You can identify some of your fears by thinking about risky or traumatic events. Try answering the following questions:

- What if I got invited to go sky-diving?
- What if I quit my job?
- What if I flew to Las Vegas tomorrow?
- What if I decided to move to a new city?
- What if my wife/husband died or left me?
- What if my parents died?

While answering these questions, try to reflect on how you feel. Do you recognize the feeling? Do you feel excited, sick, confused? Can you distinguish these from other feelings or fears?

One way to recognize career-related fears is through the use of a metaphor. Try to think of a metaphor for your workplace or your business. Is it a rat race? Is it a jungle that you have to fight through every day? Is it a house with many separate rooms? Describe this metaphor in more detail. For example, are there hurdles? What or who are those hurdles? By teasing out your metaphor you will begin to uncover some of the assumptions and fears you have about your work. Once you recognize your fears, you can then reflect on them and refine them if necessary.

> *As children we are fearless. We learn to fear based on our own life's woundings, teachings and by letting our parents' and family's fears become ours. The quickest way to master fear is to face it, walk through it and take the action you fear taking. It is helpful to engage simultaneously our physical, etheric, emotional, mental and spiritual bodies in the process. The more we are able to do this, the quicker we master our fear.*
>
> *—Tanis Helliwell,*
> *Take Your Soul to Work*

Perhaps the most common overarching fear is of failure. The fear of failing relates to all our perceptions about what will likely happen in the future. These fears may be well founded or based on false assumptions that we carry around in our minds.

Being afraid of the unknown is normal. Moving from a familiar place to an unfamiliar place is definitely challenging—not just because you do not know what is ahead, but also because you fear leaving something behind.

Even though you may feel fear, you must work through those obstacles that prevent you from being the best you can be. No change means no growth.

Answer the following questions and then reflect on your answers:

- What if I try and fail?
- What if I make mistakes?
- What if my friends abandon me?
- What if I go broke?
- What if I have to sell my home?
- What if I change my mind?
- What if people dislike me?

If you don't have a problem you are not human and if you are not human that is a problem.

—Anonymous

A useful exercise is to ask, what's the worst that could happen? Once you realize that the worst is not likely to happen or that the result won't be so bad, you can begin to think more realistically about taking on risk and overcoming fears.

The following is a list created by a group of consultants. It includes some common fears and accompanying feelings. Some may resonate with you.

Fears	Accompanying feelings
People will not buy my products or services.	I feel rejected.
People question why I am doing this.	People think I am stupid.
My family does not support me.	I will be rejected by loved ones.
I might go broke.	I will be humiliated and embarrassed.

List some of your fears and accompanying feelings here:

Fears   Accompanying feelings

_____   _____

_____   _____

_____   _____

_____   _____

When reflecting on and refining your fears, it is useful to separate facts or events from your feelings about the situation. You will quickly see that the event alone might not seem scary to anyone but you. The thoughts that you attach to that particular event are the triggers for your feelings and often disclose the underlying fear.

When you feel fear you must acknowledge the feeling and try to step away from it and gain perspective. This will enable you to put it in context.

Strategy 5: Stay focussed

The final strategy in implementing your mission is to stay focussed on your vision, mission and goals. The following are some techniques to keep you focussed:

- Use positive language;
- Treat your failures as opportunities to learn;
- Allow for time and space; and
- Have courage and trust yourself.

Use positive language

The words we use are very powerful—not just to others, but to ourselves as well. They shape how we view our world, which in turn shapes our beliefs. What you say out loud and what you think registers on your subconscious mind without you even being aware of it. Therefore, it is important to use language that supports you.

For example, many people now use the word *challenge* instead of *problem* when describing a difficult situation. They might say "This is a real challenge," as opposed to "This is a real problem." By using the word *challenge* you allow yourself a greater sense of power and control, focussing on the positive as opposed to the negative.

When going about your business, try to adopt language that is positive. Avoid phrases like "I can't . . . ," "I am too old . . ." or "I don't have enough time." Select words that are positive and empower you, and repeat these affirmations to yourself to reflect the way you want to be.

Treat your failures as opportunities to learn

The ability to deal with failure is critical to success. There are countless stories about millionaires who have failed numerous times before succeeding. Perhaps the most retold story is that of Edison and his thousands of failures before creating the lightbulb. Failures are necessary and useful to your personal and professional growth.

The other irony in life is that often great things emerge from failures. Like the Post-it notes produced by 3M. The creator was trying to develop a new glue compound and in this particular experiment the glue would not stick permanently, but could re-stick a number of times without leaving any residue.

> To venture causes anxiety; not to adventure is to lose oneself.
>
> —Kierkegaard

Allow for time and space

Bob Proctor, an expert in human potential, suggests that every new idea has a gestation period. This means that it will not be a fully developed idea, ready to implement, until it has been given some time to take root.

> I know God will not give me anything I can't handle. I just wish he didn't trust me so much.
>
> —Mother Teresa

Therefore you must allow your new ideas and perceptions time to settle. Think of it as processing time or time necessary to shift thinking and feelings around. Similarly, it is often counterproductive to try to force an idea. Let it rest to find its proper place.

When you get busy with life, you sometimes forget to stop and smell the roses. It is important, every so often, to simply check in and make sure you are on the right track. Build into your schedule little ways to break out of your fast mode—even if just for a few minutes.

John Cleese: In 1999 the *New York Times* interviewed the British comedian John Cleese. He mentioned that he was in the middle of another career transition. He had a successful career with Monty Python and later established a training company. The newspaper states: "Mr. Cleese is intent on remaining among those who do enjoy themselves, but he is taking some tortoise time to decide precisely what his next steps will be. 'The truth is, I don't know where I go now. If you try to plan with your hare brain, you'll think along the lines of what you have done before. The only way that you find a slightly new direction at this kind of juncture is to create a space and see what flows into it.' "

> *Many of life's failures are people who did not realize how close they were to success when they gave up.*
> —Thomas Edison

Although you can create a mission statement fairly quickly, it comes alive with the addition of time. The adoption and integration of your mission statement can take anywhere from a few weeks to a few months. Indeed, the true test of a mission is time. All of my learning on missions suggests that time is a critical and often overlooked aspect. Like a seed that is planted, an idea has a germination period, and as it begins to grow it will change its shape. Over time your mission will evolve. It will likely not change dramatically, but it will begin to mold to you and feel more and more comfortable. Because much of your personal programming has taken years to crystallize, it will take a while to reconfigure. Please give yourself the benefit of time. Keep what you have learned in the back of your mind, and the questions about your mission in the forefront. The answers will come over time.

Have courage and trust yourself

Courage is a skill that you can develop. It is not fearlessness. It does not mean that you are not afraid, but rather, it is the skill of dealing with the sensation of fear and overcoming it a bit at a time until you increase your capacity for situations that might evoke fear.

Learn to trust your gut feeling and listen to your emotions. We have been trained to use our brain but not our other senses. There are many books that tell us about how we use only a portion of our abilities. The recent study of emotional and spiritual intelligence deals with the same topic.

Synopsis

Even if you have a powerful mission, there is a possibility that it might fail. Some reasons are internal; some are external. This chapter introduced five strategies to help ensure that your mission becomes a reality.

The first is to integrate your vision and mission into your life. In simple terms this means reviewing them regularly and revising them when necessary.

The second strategy is to identify and take advantage of your supports—both personal and professional.

The third is to adopt appropriate attitudes. Those attitudes that hold you back must be recognized, reflected upon and refined. Specific attitudes that must be considered relate to self-esteem, money, power and success. The exercises in this chapter were designed to help you uncover and address your attitudes.

The fourth strategy is to face your fears. This means understanding where they originate and dealing with them directly.

The final strategy is to stay focussed. This includes using positive language, treating your failures as successes, allowing for time and space, having courage and trusting yourself.

If you adopt these five strategies, your mission will flourish.

When we are pursuing our Right Livelihood, even the most difficult and demanding aspects of our work will not sway us from our course. When others say, "Don't work so hard" or "Don't you ever take a break?" we will respond in bewilderment. What others may see as duty, pressure or tedium, we perceive as a kind of pleasure. Commitment is easy when our work is Right Livelihood.

—Marsha Sinetar

CONCLUSION

Living Your Mission

What will you do with this garden that has been
entrusted to you?

—Antonio Machado

At the beginning of this book I promised that by the end you would possess in your hand four 3x5 cue cards with the following titles. Blank cards are included for this purpose.

VISION	VESSEL	MISSION	GOALS
Your ideal life	What makes you unique	What you wish to accomplish	How you will achieve your mission

As you progressed through each of the chapters you were asked to fill in each of the cards with the information you gleaned by reading the book and completing the exercises. You were then asked to review them and revise them until they felt right.

If you did not fill them in as you were reading the book, you might want to do it now. As you continue your journey and grow, you should review the strategies again and refine the information until your own unique picture emerges.

In order to realize the benefit of all that you have learned, you must begin to live your vision and mission. This means reviewing

> *Go confidently in the direction of your dream. Act as though it were impossible to fail.*
>
> —Dorothea Brandt

these cards regularly, integrating the ideas into your belief system, and working and living in line with your mission.

You will be able to use your mission statement to keep you on course and to measure your success. It will help you decide what you want to do and what you do not. You can determine the extent to which your work or life is congruent with your values and ideals.

Eventually, living and working in alignment with your mission will become second nature. You will know what you are doing and why and will be able to explain this to others with confidence and ease. You will be living consciously toward the realization of your dreams.

Bibliography

Austin, Linda. *What's Holding You Back? Eight Critical Choices for Women's Success.* New York: Basic Books, 2000.

Bendaly, Leslie. *Winner Instinct: The 6 New Laws of Success.* Toronto: HarperCollins, 1999.

Bolles, Richard N. *What Color is Your Parachute?* Berkeley, CA: Ten Speed Press, 1997.

Cameron, Julia. *The Artist's Way.* New York: Penguin Putnam, 1992.

Canfeild, Jack and Jacqueline Miller. *Heart at Work: Stories and Strategies for Building Self-Esteem and Reawakening the Soul at Work.* New York: McGraw Hill, 1998.

Coombs, Ann. *The Living Workplace: Soul, Spirit, and Success in the 21st Century.* Toronto: HarperCollins, 2001.

Covey, Stephen R. *The 7 Habits of Highly Effective People.* New York: Simon & Schuster, 1989.

Covey, Stephen R., A. R. Merrill and R. Merrill. *First Things First, To Live, to Love, to Leave a Legacy.* New York: Simon & Schuster, 1995.

Gawain, Shakti. *Creating True Prosperity.* Novato, CA: New World Library, 1997.

Helliwell, Tanis. *Take Your Soul to Work: Transform Your Life and Work.* Toronto: Random House, 1999.

Hill, Napoleon. *Think and Grow Rich.* Toronto: Random House, 1960.

Jones, Laurie Beth. *The Path: Creating Your Mission Statement for Work and Life.* New York: Hyperion, 1996.

Leider, Richard and David A. Shapiro. *Repacking Your Bags: Lighten Your Load for the Rest of Your Life.* San Francisco: Berrett-Koehler, 1995.

Sher, Barbara. *It's Only Too Late If You Don't Start Now.* New York: Balantine Books, 1998.

Sher, Barbara. *Wishcraft: How to Get What you Really Want*. New York: Ballantine Books, 1979.

Sinetar, Marsha. *Do What You Love, the Money will Follow*. New York: Dell Publishing, 1987.

Stanfield, R. Brian. *The Courage to Lead: Transform Self, Transform Society*. Gabriola Island, B.C.: New Society Publishers, 2000.

Williams, Nick. *The Work We Were Born to Do: Find the Work You Love, Love the Work You Do*. Dorset, U.K.: Element, 1999.

Whyte, David. *Crossing the Unknown Sea: Work as a Pilgrimage of Identity*. New York: Riverhead Books, 2001.

Contact the Author

Keynotes and seminars
Maureen Fitzgerald is a thought-provoking and energizing speaker. She provides customized conference keynotes and in-house seminars to various groups including large corporations, associations and educational institutions. Her content is both entertaining and immediately useful for those wishing to reach new levels of productivity and success. Maureen also provides mentoring to senior managers, executives and professionals.

To contact Maureen Fitzgerald for your next conference or in-house event, please e-mail: **mfitzgerald@primus.ca**

We want your stories and feedback
Maureen would love to hear how this book has impacted your life. Do you have any stories or experiences that you would like to share? Do you have any comments on the book? Please send stories and comments to Maureen and she will make every effort to respond with a personal note. Please send them to **mfitzgerald@primus.ca**

To order more copies
To order more copies of this book, send an email to **mfitzgerald@primus.ca** or go to **www.thefitzgeraldgroup.ca.**

VISION
Your ideal life

VESSEL
What makes you unique

MISSION
What you wish to accomplish

GOALS
How you will achieve your mission